GHOST STORIES

Footprints Series
Jane Errington, Editor

The life stories of individual women and men who were participants in interesting events help nuance larger historical narratives, at times reinforcing those narratives, at other times contradicting them. The Footprints series introduces extraordinary Canadians, past and present, who have led fascinating and important lives at home and throughout the world.

The series includes primarily original manuscripts but may consider the English-language translation of works that have already appeared in another language. The editor of the series welcomes inquiries from authors. If you are in the process of completing a manuscript that you think might fit into the series, please contact her, care of McGill-Queen's University Press, 1010 Sherbrooke Street West, Suite 1720, Montreal, QC, H3A 2R7.

15 *Georges and Pauline Vanier*
Portrait of a Couple
Mary Frances Coady

16 *Blitzkrieg and Jitterbugs*
College Life in Wartime, 1939–1942
Elizabeth Hillman Waterston

17 *Harrison McCain*
Single-Minded Purpose
Donald J. Savoie

18 *Discovering Confederation*
A Canadian's Story
Janet Ajzenstat

19 *Expect Miracles*
Recollections of a Lucky Life
David M. Culver with Alan Freeman

20 *Building Bridges*
Victor C. Goldbloom

21 *Call Me Giambattista*
A Personal and Political Journey
John Ciaccia

22 *Smitten by Giraffe*
My Life as a Citizen Scientist
Anne Innis Dagg

23 *The Oil Has Not Run Dry*
The Story of My Theological Pathway
Gregory Baum

24 *My Peerless Story*
It Starts with the Collar
Alvin Cramer Segal

25 *Wrestling with Life*
From Hungary to Auschwitz to Montreal
George Reinitz with Richard King

26 *Never Rest on Your Ores*
Building a Mining Company, One Stone at a Time
Norman B. Keevil

27 *The Making of a Museum*
Judith Nasby

28 *Gold's Rounds*
Medicine, McGill, and Growing Up Jewish in Montreal
Phil Gold

29 *Ghost Stories*
On Writing Biography
Judith Adamson

GHOST STORIES

On Writing Biography

Judith Adamson

McGill-Queen's University Press
Montreal & Kingston • London • Chicago

© McGill-Queen's University Press 2024

ISBN 978-0-2280-2103-2 (paper)
ISBN 978-0-2280-2156-8 (ePDF)
ISBN 978-0-2280-2157-5 (ePUB)

Legal deposit second quarter 2024
Bibliothèque nationale du Québec

Printed in Canada on acid-free paper that is 100% ancient forest free (100% post-consumer recycled), processed chlorine free

Funded by the Government of Canada | Financé par le gouvernement du Canada | Canada | Canada Council for the Arts | Conseil des arts du Canada

We acknowledge the support of the Canada Council for the Arts.
Nous remercions le Conseil des arts du Canada de son soutien.

McGill-Queen's University Press in Montreal is on land which long served as a site of meeting and exchange amongst Indigenous Peoples, including the Haudenosaunee and Anishinabeg nations. In Kingston it is situated on the territory of the Haudenosaunee and Anishinaabek. We acknowledge and thank the diverse Indigenous Peoples whose footsteps have marked these territories on which peoples of the world now gather.

Library and Archives Canada Cataloguing in Publication

Title: Ghost stories : on writing biography / Judith Adamson.
Names: Adamson, Judith, author.
Series: Footprints series (Montréal, Quebec) ; 29.
Description: Series statement: Footprints series ; 29 | Includes bibliographical references and index.
Identifiers: Canadiana (print) 20230581439 | Canadiana (ebook) 20230581498 | ISBN 9780228021032 (paper) | ISBN 9780228021575 (EPUB) | ISBN 9780228021568 (EPDF)
Subjects: LCSH: Adamson, Judith. | LCSH: Women biographers—Canada—Biography. | LCSH: Biographers—Canada—Biography. | LCSH: Biography as a literary form. | LCGFT: Autobiographies.
Classification: LCC CT34.C3 A33 2024 | DDC 920.071—dc23

For my grandchildren,
Andrew and Bronwyn

Contents

Prologue

About halfway through the pandemic lockdown I took up *This Long Pursuit*, Richard Holmes's reflections on writing biography. When he finished his first book, about Percy Bysshe Shelley, Holmes concluded that biographers should follow two rules, the "Footsteps principle" and the "Two-Sided Notebook concept." I was writing about Jean Ross at the time, the real Sally Bowles of Christopher Isherwood's *Goodbye to Berlin* but, being interested in Holmes's conclusions, I put it aside to look through the notebooks of my own biographical research. They were not so neatly organized as Holmes's sounded. On the right side of his, he had recorded the objective facts he accumulated while following his subjects' past footsteps, and on the left his personal responses to what he found. Still, one way or another, I had done a similar kind of "double accounting."

On the opening page of my working notes from the day I first met Graham Greene in October 1970, at a time when he rarely granted interviews, I had written in capital letters "NO TAPE RECORDER ALLOWED." Many pages and personal annotations later I'd scribbled in the margin: "He made me drink an enormous vodka martini with no ice before we went to lunch, and too much wine at lunch. Why? I don't know how I stayed alert. He drank much more and talked until 7. No tape recorder proved a huge asset." I'm sure what I came to call my trial by martini is what led to his interest in my work and prompted me to write my first biography, a political one about him. Some years later we chose the essays together for *Reflections*, the last of his books published in his lifetime. Since his death I have added some essays to its second edition. In my "double accounting" I found he had told his longtime publisher Max Reinhardt that my introduction was the best essay in the book. Beside that comment I had scribbled "untrue."

In my notebooks I found descriptions of the hard work of biographical writing that followed, and of my teaching at Dawson College in Montreal all the while. There were stories about people who helped me write, sometimes in unexpected ways, like prize-winning designer Sigrun Bülow-Hübe and writer Vincent Brome, who encouraged so many scholars in the British Library.

And I discovered things I'd forgotten, the ghost stories of memory. A Montreal dinner party had led me to hunt down the private correspondence between Leonard Woolf and Trekkie Ritchie Parsons; the sometimes intimate conversations I'd had with Trekkie's Sussex friends had earned me their trust to publish it. I found comments about how impressed I had been with the old members of the British Communist Party I'd met at the home of historian George Rudé and his wife, Doreen, in Rye. They had encouraged me to write Charlotte Haldane's story. And I unearthed many, many personal notes of my friendship with Max Reinhardt, notes that had enabled me to write his biography.

But even as I captured their biographical likenesses, I knew that however much I tried to get out of the way, their stories were mine on the page. Like a metaphor, each biography is what it is and something else, a written life and an imprint of the biographer. Comprehension depends on where you stand. So, as I continued to search my notes for clues about how I had managed that balance in order to produce a lively sense of the person whose life I was recreating, the questions I'd asked myself and the personal challenges I'd faced, I began to write this book about the cumulative experience of the biographical process. From the start I knew it had to include the hidden side of the conundrum – the biographer, who is both writer and first reader of the book, and who is inevitably changed by the enterprise.

We live in stories. At first these are other people's stories that become ours as we search for our own sense of the world. Then they change, sometimes with deranging speed, sometimes so gradually that we don't notice until later. Many of our stories are without words. Yet even they belong to someone else long before death takes possession of us, if we're lucky. My story is not that of the people whose biographies I wrote, but in writing theirs I found mine. As Alan Bennett said to his filmed doppelganger at the end of *The Lady in the Van*, "You don't put yourself into what you write. You find yourself there." It happened this way. Just keep in mind that this account bears the bias of my place and generation.

GHOST STORIES

1

Coming of Age

Montreal snow squeaks under my boots on the iron staircase to the street. I am four and an easy target for the French kids across Third Avenue in Rosemount. They shout something about the war that I don't understand and the snowball I throw has no muscle. Theirs hits me on the head. "Tête carrée!" they shriek as I round the corner onto Bellechasse. "Maudits Anglais."

It's just another morning. A sunny one for a change and I'm warm in my British wool coat with its blue velvet collar. Three or four blocks along Bellechasse is Nesbitt School, where I'd been expelled from kindergarten in September for sneaking out of class and hiding in the surrounding field until it was time to go home. Hence the letter I threw under the stairs that snaked up to our second-floor flat. I couldn't read it but I knew it spelled trouble, and even in ambush the French kids never went under those stairs. I had two mornings entirely to myself, watching azure cornflowers wave at the autumn sky. They were the most beautiful things I'd seen, other than the windows in the United Church across Rosemount Boulevard on the Sunday side of the school. The advantage there was music. Then came the principal's phone call, my two-week expulsion from kindergarten, and the beginning of my Nesbitt School reputation.

I caught a lot of stones in those days. The French kids were older than me and they knew a thing or two about playing hookey. My mother's punishments were British. There were smacks. There was the hairbrush and, if her hands were full, the adamant kick. When she was really tired she'd put me in the kitchen cupboards under the counter. Not a smidgeon of triumph in that, but she was otherwise powerless, alone with me and my little brother while my father worked late for the war effort. Even with one of her two older sisters and often her parents down the street, she was defeated. Brought away at twelve from her Bradford-on-Avon school, where she'd played field hockey and collected flowers that she painted with precision, to a Rosemount flat where little more than fifteen years later she listened by night to the CBC shortwave reports from the war fronts and imagined her British cousins and friends crushed by debris. She said her earliest memory was of hiding under the table while her father played the piano to calm her during the Zeppelin bombing of Sheffield on 26 September 1916. When I could read, one of her schoolmates sent me *Hereward the Wake* and *The Water Babies*. Perhaps they'd read Charles Kingsley together. Or were the books thanks for the food packages my mother sent her well into the fifties? The war news frightened me too with its grim descriptions and battleground sounds. And I was terrified under the counter, banging the saucepan lids together to break the dark.

My mother and her parents were the last of her immediate family to immigrate. Montreal would cure her father's asthma, the Wiltshire doctor had advised. But what of hers? So unconscious that autumn that they thought her dead until the undertaker said she was not and sent for an ambulance. That too I heard and saw. But perhaps it was the next year when I was in first grade that I came home from school in the afternoon to find the flat full of people who tried to stop me from seeing her.

She seemed dead to me, although at four or five I knew nothing about death except from the war reports. It certainly didn't answer when I talked to it, or put its arm around me when I stretched my body beside it on the bed. Dead meant I was sent up the street to my cousins' house and only told the next day that my mother was in the hospital where children could not visit, but my aunt would sneak me in to prove her point. That was after taking me and my cousins to see *The Wizard of Oz* as a treat. It was my first film and when the witch rose on the screen I screamed until they took me out. My terror was added to the list of my misdemeanours and everyone was in a very dark mood when we crept up the hospital's back stairs to find my mother, alive or dead.

Did my transgressions warrant the punishments? Oh yes, my cousins both say. Under those blond curls and behind that pretty face there was knowledge and defiance. I hid beneath the stairs the butter that accidentally fell from the bag of rations I was sent to buy at the corner store, and claimed that what I brought home was what the shopkeeper had given me. I pushed down the sewer the lid of the Pyrex bowl I dropped returning it to my aunt, and lied that it hadn't been sent. I punched in the window of her front door when my cousins didn't answer the bell and the French kids had chased me down the street with their stones. I still have the scar so perilously close to the veins on my inner left wrist that doctors sometimes look at it and wonder if I once had a suicidal intention. I badly cut my brother's right thumb pulling away the knife my mother had left within his grasp on his high chair when she hurried to answer the phone. I got tar on my new green dress in the forbidden lumber yard beside our flat the day a photographer came to take our family portrait. Even then I didn't trust prettiness and always scowled when asked to smile for a camera. Or perhaps it was my only power against unfairness.

Not accidents, my cousins say. It was my naughtiness that made them lock me in the chicken coop on our uncle's meagre Barrington farm an hour's drive south of Montreal, day after day, the summer I was five. No one believed me until he heard me crying at the window. He let me out all right, and to cure me of my fear held me roughly by the arm at the back of the barn, strung a chicken upside down on a nail, and forced me to hold the knife under his hand while we slit the chicken's throat.

When I told this story to the writer Vincent Brome over lunch at the British Library decades later to explain my fear of the pigeons in Russell Square, he read the scene in the Freudian way he read everything, the chicken's neck being ... you know the rest. I'm sure he was wrong, although I have no memory of running back to the farmhouse splattered in blood. Only of running for my life. Memory is such an invasive thing. It folds the present into the future, and then the past. So, where is the present when the past pops up like a puppet in a Punch and Judy show to hit us on the head?

My grandmother's sister lived on Fifth Avenue above Bellechasse where it merged with Fourth, that street ending there. Her garden backed onto my aunt's on Third Avenue. It was filled with enough vegetables for many months to come. Only a dirt lane separated their rough wooden fences but we were rarely allowed across it alone. There was a fierce petty bourgeois competition between them. They sometimes even argued over who was older. In the triplex beside her lived one of my great-aunt's daughters with her husband and deaf son. He had blond hair and large searching eyes, and his nose was always running. I loved that boy. He loved me too and he couldn't understand any more than I could why I sometimes shook him when I took him for walks in his stroller. He was two and I was five and one shameful day I slapped him until his eyes brimmed with tears. I was told never to take him out of his pushcart but his crying gave me an excuse to and there was solace in clinging to one another in the street until we both stopped sobbing. People said he had no hearing because his mother had left him on the outside landing in the winter and his brains froze.

His aunt lived a few doors further along Fifth Avenue. She was talked about by grownups in hushed tones. She had a daughter, two sons, and a French husband who hanged himself after forcing her to whore in their flat. Downtown Montreal was racy in the forties and

I guess a living could be had by staging sex shows even in Rosemount. The *maudits Anglais* were accused of wealth but she was dirt poor like the rest of us. My mother stood up for her. But her husband left a note when he hanged himself saying it was his wife's idea. She went to jail for many years, the children to foster care.

A few weeks after I started third grade my teacher summoned me to the front and, prattling praise, announced that I was moving to the Town of Mount Royal. I knew instinctively there was something wrong with my elevation from school villain to favoured child. But there it was. A clean split to a new enclave of houses above the south-east corner of the Town where the Canadian National Railway tracks ran south under the mountain to Central Station and the Canadian Pacific tracks crossed over them carrying freight east and west. There would be no more Nesbitt School record, no French kids to throw stones, no accusing cousins down the street, no Fifth Avenue squalor to be whispered about. The war was over. Having just turned eight I was given another chance.

✿✿✿

I wouldn't want to rewrite this genius loci using Ian McEwan's "it might have been." Life is inartistic. And it wasn't all black. There were family picnics in Barrington. And seamless days there with my cousins dressing kittens in dolls' clothes and walking them around the farmyard in an old baby carriage. There was berry picking. When my mother and her sisters fired up the wood stove to bake pies, everyone was happy. When they cooked a chicken there were innards to examine under the kitchen table and, when it rained, Eaton's catalogues to look at under the farmhouse stairs. In Rosemount there were piano lessons advised by a spunky teenager named Maureen Forrester, who became one of the world's leading contraltos. She sang with my mother's best friend in a downtown church choir and told me she wanted to be a band singer at Danceland above Dinty

Moore's on Ste Catherine Street. She said my four-year-old singing voice had tone and volume and was entirely off key. I had big hands. The piano would train my ear.

It didn't, but I played it with pleasure for years and so well that when I was examined at seven I topped all the teenagers widely in marks. The examiner was Osborne Peasgood, the sub-organist at Westminister Abbey. I made mistakes with my scales and arpeggios that morning at McGill until he sat with me on the piano bench and said he'd been nervous when he played at the coronation of King George VI and at Princess Elizabeth's wedding. He encouraged a simple duet. Then I played some Bach from *Anna Magdalena's Notebook* for him, a Mozart waltz, and the first scene of Schumann's *Kinderszenen*, which he asked me to sight read. He gave me two tickets to his concert at the church of St Andrew and St Paul and that evening told my mother I had a career ahead. But she was pragmatic, and a month before I began high school my lessons were stopped.

Because of my mother's asthma I was often sent to stay with her parents in the country. They had rented a stone house surrounded by lilac and meadow a few miles from the Barrington farm. After my grandfather died I used to sleep on the inside of my grandmother's bed beside the wall. She read me Blake and Wordsworth from *A Child's Garden of Verses* and the whole of *The Secret Garden* and *Jane Eyre*. She told me stories about England. Did she have an English accent? I only remember that her reading voice was gentle. She took me once to a small brick church where I played with other children on the floor under a quilting frame and listened to the ribald happenings the farm wives told one another as they laughed and stitched away their afternoon. When evening fell and we walked out into the snow holding hands, my grandmother said almost secretly, "Memories are what we're made of. Today you heard happy ones."

She was late-Victorian, her long grey hair always knotted up and, except in bed, her flesh-coloured corset wrapped around her thin body. She could darn a sock so finely it looked new and skin an apple in one piece so the peel stood up as though still holding fruit. She argued with my father about politics. When he thought he'd won, she'd fire her final volley as she left the room, invariably shattering his argument. I last saw her when I was in my mid-twenties and she in her mid-nineties. She said she was an anachronism. She'd been in Trafalgar Square when the twentieth century was ushered in and made me promise to be there at the dawn of the twenty-first. I got there one day late and braved the pigeons with two sturdy umbrellas to cross from St Martin-in-the-Fields to Canada House.

Like me, my father was born in Rosemount. In his adolescence he walked miles every day to Montreal High School on University Street just above Sherbrooke, saving his streetcar fare for the movies. He ranked first each year but no relative ever came to see him handed his medals and there were no scholarships to McGill for working-class students. Instead of becoming a lawyer, he took a job at the Windsor Hotel and accountancy classes, the only ones given at night. It must have been in 1944 that he memorized Quebec's Civil Code. When he came home late in Rosemount he used to wake me to keep him company while he ate his supper. If he was very hungry he would break two boiled eggs into a white bowl, the yolks running yellow. Then he would place the deep blue, leather-bound Code in my hands and recite it to me as though it were a bedtime story, turning the pages I couldn't read.

His mother had come from Newfoundland. He said her father was a banker and that when he died her brothers ran off leaving her penniless. It seemed an unlikely story to me until I met her uncle, who had a shock of white hair, genteel manners, and a vermillion velvet smoking jacket. Emily died just before I was born. My middle name is hers, and when my father placed on his dresser a photograph of me at eighteen beside the only one he had of her, you could hardly tell the difference between us. She must have met her husband at the Plymouth Brethren hall where she took their children twice on Sundays and on Wednesday evenings too. My father said the reason he'd done so well in school was that he hid his Latin book behind his Bible and memorized Virgil and Ovid.

His father's family had come from a small fishing village in Scotland named Ferryden. They fled bad times and fell on bad times. In Montreal, his father cleaned the inside of gasoline tanks. Perhaps it was the fumes that made him so vicious. He used to beat his four children regularly. My father hated him and detested religion. I've seen people die but none with the fear I saw in my father's eyes, which could only have come from the early Plymouth Brethren horrors he'd tried to banish by memorizing Latin as a boy.

I don't know where he found the money to get us out of Rosemount. He may have borrowed it from his friend Sam Krasnow, a jeweller whose books he kept. Uncle Sam, as we used to call him, came often for supper and close to Christmas with new one-dollar bills to give us our share of the Chanukah gelt he took to all the children he knew. He once invited me to his mother's flat for dessert after Shabbat dinner. Her rooms were full of paintings and intricately patterned carpets, the table laden with candles and cakes and a silver samovar. It was a mysterious and delicious place. She encouraged me to play her piano and read me short poems that fused my heightened senses into words. Or perhaps it was not Sam but the bank who loaned my father the mortgage money on his own rising expectations. From the war on, he worked for Vapor Heating Corporation, a company that began by making industrial boilers. He rose in it as it expanded through the fifties and sixties, to become vice-president of the American conglomerate that bought it in the 1980s.

✪✪✪

Like so many others built in Montreal in the early postwar years, 7375 de Roquancourt was a semi-detached brick house. The neighbourhood was geographically cut off from the city by the Canadian Pacific train tracks that ran east and west through the woods at the top of our street. So we went to Carlyle School and used the other community facilities of the then almost entirely English Town of Mount Royal. Unlike those of the Town itself, our neighbourhood streets bore both French and English war names, of which de Roquancourt was the hardest to spell and pronounce. Before my mother let me loose she made me repeat it over and over in case I got lost, which was unlikely since I'd already mastered a large swath of Rosemount.

She considered the house hers to display and a communal responsibility to care for. Many neighbours had cleaners and a few had an extra car but there was no money in our family for such indulgence. My parents were good with their hands and my mother's English manners made up for some of the class discrepancy between them and their more-established neighbours. A doer with many practical talents, she remained uneasy gossiping over coffee with the de Roquancourt women and lonely away from her sister and church-centred social life. It took her years to lose her sense of insecurity.

Although I loathed my assigned chores, they made me handy. As soon as we moved from Rosemount I was taught to measure and inject her adrenalin subcutaneously in case she couldn't breathe. This was an exacting responsibility for a child and I carried it out several times a year, once when I found her unconscious in the kitchen. Every Saturday I waxed hardwood floors on my knees and made a game of polishing them by sliding about in my thickest socks until I was chastened for making play out of work. I never had a store-bought dress until I was twelve and was taught to make my own clothes long before that. I darned socks and knitted scarves, dug the herbaceous borders and helped plant the hedges at the back of the house, the perennial beds in front. In winter my brother and I shovelled plenty of snow. When the chores were done, my mother was happy to be rid of me. She believed in fresh air and cod liver oil, delivered on a tablespoon each morning at breakfast, to be followed by freshly squeezed orange juice. An allergist had told her this would save us from getting her asthma.

Between the ages of eight and twelve I biked endlessly with my girlfriends and farther than we were allowed. Once it was miles down Côte-des-Neiges, east along Sherbrooke through city traffic to the Jacques Cartier Bridge, and halfway across it to St Helen's Island in the St Lawrence River to picnic on apples. We played jacks on our driveways and made up plays we performed in our garages. In winter we took painting classes at the town hall and learned to figure skate on the rink at the end of the street. When we were a little older we played hockey, won the Montreal Girls' Championship, and sat on park benches winter and summer to share secrets and begin to imagine life for ourselves. De Roquancourt was a good place to spend one's elementary school years. It became constricting when my mother's 1950s aspirations for me began to close in.

I remember only one catastrophe in that house, when I was nine and my mother told me my father didn't care about us anymore. He was having an affair with his secretary. By then I was well acquainted with unconsciousness; affairs sounded much worse. Since she had no money she'd have to get a job and a flat and leave me and my brother somewhere during the week, she thought with the nuns on Decelles Avenue. There was a building there on the corner of Côte-Sainte-Catherine that she pointed out every time we passed. It was where "bad girls" went to have babies the nuns took away. In my English Protestant mind nuns were French Catholic. They didn't throw stones like the Rosemount boys; they stole babies. In her misery she cried on and on, and when my father came home there was a dreadful row in the kitchen behind the closed door. Through my tears I couldn't hear much of it. It was something about an unspoken contract between her and the house. I suspect it had to do with her fear of falling back into the proletariat, her dream of rising to a more secure stratum of life shattered by my father's infidelity. The final sally was clear. If he didn't fire his secretary she'd tell his boss and he'd lose his job. If she ever said anything about this to me again he'd leave her and take me and my brother with him.

Graham Greene said there is always a moment in childhood when the door opens and lets the future in. After that day my father seemed less confident, his voice diminished. And I was changed too. From then on he usually deferred to my mother. From then on I never trusted her. Probably I had never trusted her since the day she nearly died, but that was a different kind of betrayal. Perhaps my father just grew old on that day, and I grew up. Or perhaps the pattern was in the carpet all along and Rosemount çaught up with us both.

From then on I somehow knew why the French kids had thrown stones at me. France had made a deal with Hitler so that when Hitler bombed the *maudits Anglais* in England, they were doing their bit for France in Montreal. Mussolini had protected the Italian boys down the street from their stones, but seeing my father's youngest brother and his friends coming up to our flat in their military uniforms had made me an easy English target. And the Jewish people? The nuns and priests had said they killed Jesus and the Société Saint-Jean-Baptiste had sent a petition to Parliament urging Mackenzie King not to accept them as refugees. My grandmother said the Catholic Church was anti-semitic and Mackenzie King probably was too. At best he was a coward to be influenced by a petition, even one with 128,000 prominent names attached, and fickle not to enforce conscription until the war was nearly over because Quebec didn't want it.

Then there was my grade three teacher. She was poor like us but she held the Town of Mount Royal English in awe. There had always been something fishy about that sentiment. When it came to the English, the French kids made no distinction between poor and rich. I knew they were wrong to think that all the *Anglais* were *maudits*, and wrong about Hitler and Jews. Still, I disliked her more than I was hurt by their stones. I had escaped this confusion in the tabula rasa of de Roquancourt, our street on the edge of English privilege. But it was there waiting for me all the time. Knowledge of it was my Rosemount heritage, as the Plymouth Brethren and social deprecation were my father's. I talked. He went silent. Life went on and I grew independent as young people do if given the chance.

My father finished the basement and expanded the kitchen. My mother was at her best with her hands in the earth. As long as they worked together on her tireless house improvements they seemed content. In spite of her asthma she had enormous energy and a 1950s aspirant zeal. The words "housewife" and "prisoner" had not yet become synonymous to her. When there was nothing else to be done, she wanted to move. This we did when I was in eighth grade, to a larger house on the western margin of the Town where her busy pattern of furbishment continued. That second house backed onto a Jewish cemetery. For a couple of years there was a field between our lawn and any graves. It was my River Styx and I crossed it often to walk among the dead, whose faces were sealed in their tombstones under glass.

In eighth grade at the Town of Mount Royal High School I made two new friends. The mother of one was connected with a small private school in Westmount. St George's was based on A.S. Neill's Summerhill in England. My mother heard "England" and ranked the school with velvet-collared coats, Oxford shoes, and the "better people" she thought I'd meet there. She'd never heard of Summerhill or progressive education. St George's only went up to ninth grade at the time and had decided to take in a few new pupils so that it could graduate its first class in 1958. I went with my friends to write an entrance exam I think was an IQ test. We were all admitted, myself on half fees of $200 a year.

There were seven of us in the class and nine in the group below. We had two rooms to ourselves at the back of the third of three old houses on the corner of Westmount Boulevard and Ramezay Road. The younger children had classes in the first two houses. The janitor and his wife, who cooked our lunches, lived in ours, as did the principal, Agnes Matthews, and her poodle, Susie. She taught us Latin and we took our classes sitting on the floor of her office. It was not our favourite subject and we often played tricks on her, once tying her shoe laces together under her desk as we read our translations aloud. With its nooks and crannies and huge garden where we played baseball and skated, the building felt as much like her home as our school. There was disorder everywhere and more books than I'd ever seen. We read and wrote and talked, went to the theatre, concerts, and exhibitions. Mario Duschenes taught us to play the recorder and played Bach for us on his flute. By Christmas I was both socialist and atheist and argued as passionately as my grandmother. St George's wasn't the ordinary private school my mother had expected and she wanted me out. But here my father spoke up and her only recourse was to upbraid this child who had already chosen things very different from what she wanted for her. "I can't argue with you anymore," she conceded. "You have words." My kid brother, however, would remain in the Town of Mount Royal school.

✪✪✪

About that time my parents bought from a friend an acre of land on Lake Champlain where the Richelieu River meets it very close to the American border. The farmer whose land it was lived in the United Empire Loyalist house of his ancestors. It had an attached storage barn with an attic full of farm and war relics going back to the early nineteenth century. On rainy days I went up there with his children to sit on sacks of dried corn and read old ledgers and diaries. On sunny ones we swam or rowed the mile and a half across the lake to Fort Montgomery near Rouses Point. It had been erected between 1844 and 1871 to replace what the locals still call Fort Blunder, a smaller structure accidentally built on the Canadian side of the border twenty-five years earlier. At Fort Montgomery we explored the derelict limestone arches that had once led to the officers' quarters and the remaining bastions whose only light came through rifle slits. Stairs ended in bottomless black holes or led up to rotting roofs overgrown with grass grazed by cows. I found a cannon ball with a fossilized leaf in one of the bastions and used it for a door stop. My father built a small summer cottage while my mother tamed the field into lawn, dug and planted more gardens, and started a cedar hedge with trees that my brother and I stole for her from the woods on the American side of the border. When I set off alone for the day in my canoe or sailboat, she would simply say "be careful" as she had when I pedalled away from de Roquancourt on my bike.

My cousins now lived in Hemmingford, about thirty miles from the cottage and nearer to our uncle's Barrington farm. They had joined the Canadian Girls in Training and I was encouraged to join the group at Mount Royal United Church. It was then a huge Protestant girls' organization, larger than the Girl Guides. No knot-tying badges for us; we were supposed to be in training to be good Christians. As well as having the usual girls'-club fun, we studied the Bible, followed the travels of missionaries, and did community work. One year this included babysitting for families in Saint-Henri, the poverty-stricken setting of Gabrielle Roy's *Bonheur d'Occasion*. For my Mount Royal friends Saint-Henri was a frightening part of Montreal. For me it was Rosemount, only entirely French and poorer. I got to know one family a little. It was my first amicable experience with the Québécois. They were warm and dignified and deprived. I was embarrassed by the difference between us and felt my charity diminished them. I knew their need and they appreciated the time I spent with their children, but we both wanted a society of economic and social justice and even then I knew that middle-class do-gooders weren't the answer.

The CGIT summer camp was near Georgeville on Lake Memphremagog. I went there first when I was eleven and returned every July for a couple of weeks until I was sixteen, when I was a swimming instructor for the younger campers and stayed for two months. One breath of the fir- and flower-scented air of the Eastern Townships left me as enchanted as Wordsworth was by the Lake District. Cedar Lodge was a beautiful wild place and I still go often to the Abbaye de Saint-Benoît-du-Lac across the lake from it to listen to the Benedictine monks sing Gregorian chants and to buy their cheeses and cider. When I was fifteen I was elected CGIT vice-president for Quebec and that year spent many weekends with the president, who was a pal from Cedar Lodge, and the two women who were in charge of the organization. We travelled around the province leading Sunday church services in our middies. I was seduced by the music, the stained-glass light, the formality of peace. And I became a decent speaker. Done well, the ritual was great theatre, complete with costumes and music and adolescent me in one of the leading roles. But try as I might, I couldn't believe what I was preaching and in good Protestant conscience left it all behind before I finished high school.

⚬⚬⚬

Then came the time for decision. It was still the 1950s. Nursing or secretarial school, my mother said. Take your choice. It wasn't difficult. I was fascinated with medicine and in those days middle-class Montreal girls with that inclination almost invariably became nurses. My mother expected me to be wearing an engagement ring soon, and I suppose she thought a doctor would make a better son-in-law than my St George's School boyfriend, Peter Lebensold. One of my cousins was already engaged and I'd been sent on dates with the sons of my mother's friends. One Friday a young United Church minister took me to a party where the game was Spin the Bottle. When I saw that the penalty was more than a kiss, I left. He followed and pinned me against our garage door wanting what he'd missed. I escaped by shouting at him, but my mother didn't believe a religious fellow capable of such behaviour and carried on with her mission.

Her problem soon widened. I had passed enough subjects to get into university but had not studied chemistry or biology, both required for nursing. And although I had a good mark in geometry, I had badly failed algebra. Since I was only sixteen when I finished high school and you had to be eighteen to begin nursing, she determined that I would spend a gap year learning algebra under my father's tutelage, and chemistry and biology under the guidance of a woman she knew through her church connections who taught both subjects at Outremont High School.

Frances Wallace was frighteningly strict. "Your mother tells me you can't do math," she barked when we began. "That's utter nonsense. Just stop me if you don't understand something." And on she went for the next seven months, two hours each week, in her lab. She had grown up on a small farm in Nova Scotia where as a child her face and neck had been badly scarred in a house fire. Her first scholarship was to Dalhousie University. Another followed to Radcliffe, but the Depression forced her to leave Cambridge before she could finish her PhD. A friend got her a job teaching at a private girls' school in Montreal, where she boarded free in return for housework so she could send her small teaching salary to her family. She soon moved into the public school system because the pay was higher. Eventually she created the biology and chemistry curricula for Quebec high schools and gave lectures all over the world.

She was the finest teacher I ever encountered. In the two hours a week I spent with her that winter she taught me four years of high school chemistry and biology. Entirely to her credit, I took top place on both McGill entrance exam papers, answering by choice all the math questions offered. And that gap year held another unexpected, but not unconnected benefit. Alone in my bedroom overlooking the cemetery, I began to write – reviews of books I read, stories I made up about the people whose faces I found sealed in their tombstones, poems – all bottom-drawer stuff, but it began the habit. Frances taught me I could learn anything I wanted to, even math, and not to depend on what my mother said for my own sense of worth. In silence I learned the sheer pleasure of patterning thought on paper.

I was as lucky to know Frances as I was to have attended St George's, and to have had my narrow home view widened by Peter's Polish father. On Saturday mornings architect Fred Lebensold used to take us around the city with him to inspect the buildings he and his firm, ARCOP, had designed or were associated with. I stood on top of Place Ville Marie before it was clad in siding, and jumped gently on the stage at Place des Arts on opening night with the National Ballet's then director, Celia Franca, to feel its softness. The afternoon before that great evening I listened alone to the orchestra rehearse while Fred checked last-minute details backstage. When I sit in those crimson seats today and look up at the acoustical ceiling he called his flight of angels, I'm as enchanted as I was then. People now come in jeans but Salle Wilfrid-Pelletier still wraps them in elegance.

Though as a teenager Peter seemed apathetic about Fred's instruction, I took in a practical architectural education on those Saturday mornings, and at the Lebensolds' home on Ramezay Road listened to their cosmopolitan friends who were also reshaping Montreal. Architect Hazen Sise told me about driving Norman Bethune's mobile blood bank in the Spanish Civil War. Artist Ghitta Caiserman would talk to me about modern art if in return I played Chopin with Peter's mother. While I found my own family complacent and dull, it provided Peter with the Canadian commonness he needed. My mother cooked as his rarely did and absorbed his adolescent energy in summer cottage and other family projects rather than in the world of books and art that his family provided me. My father never discussed his work, while Fred's growing fame was always in the spotlight on Ramezay Road. Except when my grandmother was visiting, the main amusement in my house was television. And yet, and for different reasons, a few years later both families ensnared us in the same disastrous marriage plot.

As I saw it at seventeen, the widest fault line between the worlds of our families was university, and without parental encouragement I couldn't get there. My friends went to McGill. I went to the Royal Victoria Hospital, set into the mountain above the university, to be trained. By Christmas of my first year I begged release, but this time my mother won. Perhaps it was sheer tiredness with my arguments that made my father say I had to finish what I'd started. More likely it was my mother's fear of the greater distance university would put between us. Although I well knew the difference to me of being sent, however accidentally, to St George's, I didn't then understand that being there had somehow shifted me in the many layers of the middle class. Nor did I understand how going there and living in the Town of Mount Royal had for some years stretched family funds, or why in those pre-medicare years we were mostly treated with home remedies. And although I had never been held back from physical activities, I had also never been encouraged intellectually. When my mother died of pancreatic cancer within three weeks of the diagnosis, I was thirty-eight and had a PhD as well as an RN. Almost her last words to me were: "You're the girl. You have to take care of your father and brother. Don't forget. You're the girl." In her world mothers trained their daughters to be helpmeets.

At the Royal Victoria Hospital we lived in the attached nurses' residence and were either in class or working on the wards eight hours a day, often eight of each. Probably because the school was militaristic, the training was excellent and the hospital patient-care focused in a way almost unimaginable today. We underwent tedious drudgery in those three years and took on skilled medical responsibility well beyond our age, although not our capability. We were given a solid grounding in the health sciences. After a few months I could name every bone and muscle in the body as well as splint breaks and bandage tears. I knew the basics of physiology and biochemistry and pretty soon of psychiatry, pediatrics, and neurology. A red Coke machine stood beside the door to the hospital morgue. I watched autopsies there several times a month. I delivered babies, held retractors and organs in the operating theatres, and stitched incisions. I once took out someone's appendix. Not all my classmates did these things, and some of them we were not supposed to do. But if we were interested and capable the resident doctors usually obliged. And, not by choice, I spent a month at the Allan Memorial Institute with the patients in Ewen Cameron's electroshock ward. So gruesome was that place that at Christmas, when the inmates had been reduced to childhood, a fellow student and I stole a decorated tree from the hospital's front lobby and carried it up Pine Avenue in a blizzard to cheer them, and ourselves.

Nursing was then a proud and respected profession, and the school at the Royal Vic was among the best in the world. But hospital life was limiting. Many of my classmates spent their free time hunting for husbands in McGill's fraternity houses. I went to the McGill Film

Society with Peter and his friends Adam Symansky and Ronnie Blumer, both of whom became distinguished filmmakers. There I first watched Sergei Eisenstein and Ingmar Bergman, whose films marked me deeply. With a couple of musical classmates, one who played a classical guitar and the other a flute, I took up my recorders to play at one of our teachers' dinner parties. She had friends in the city's choral circles and for a short time we were passed from party to party. There I met Maureen Forrester again and her pals George Little, music director of the Erskine and American Church, and Gifford Mitchell, who directed the Montreal Elgar Choir. I walked the old city for hours with Heather Jamieson, my closest Royal Vic friend, imagining we were in Europe and discussing our futures. She decided the way forward was travel; I enrolled in a night course at Sir George Williams College, where Rachel Wasserman talked about the cultural history of Western civilization.

As the three years passed I found hospital work increasingly tiresome. We were hierarchically disciplined and undervalued until the McGill University–trained nurses began to impose themselves on the wards and everyone admitted our superior medical knowledge and efficiency. Of the 150 of us who began in September 1958 only half graduated. The others failed or dropped out without recognition. At our five-day-long licensing exams we were rightly warned that in medicine there is no room for error. Marks were deducted for wrong answers.

In my last summer some of us who made it through were put into white uniforms early to top up the staff. We'd been running the wards for years in pink and white stripes and I happily accepted the graduate disguise for a small remuneration. I've always appreciated the medical skills I ended up with, but not their conjoined professional numbness. I had held too many suffering hands, shared too many dying words, gained too little wisdom. After pocketing what I earned that summer I packed my starched whites, took a deep breath, and fled down the hill in a black skirt and turtleneck sweater.

✪✪✪

In 1962 the back door of Sir George Williams College opened onto Stanley Street. Hungarian immigrants had made coffee houses there for themselves and a campus for us. While my McGill friends sat under their lofty trees dismissing us as intellectually suspicious, I drank my first espresso in the Pam-Pam. The croissant came with butter and jam, and we honours English students took breakfast there every morning for the next three years. Suppers were often at the Rose Marie, where black bean soup and a plate of stuffed cabbage or mushroom goulash could be had for ninety-nine cents. If short of cash, students were usually fed anyway. Like most immigrants, the Hungarians valued education. Then it was up the street to the Carmen, where Vilallonga's murals adorned the restaurant walls, musicians played their guitars, and poets recited their work while cigarettes were butted in overflowing ashtrays and talk went late into the night.

Stanley and Mountain Streets formed the geography of our imaginations, the centre of our songs and novels and poems. When not in their coffee houses our base was the English table in the library. There we read of T.S. Eliot's Phlebas, who "was once handsome and tall" as us, of Christopher Marlowe's Faustus, who found heaven in a kiss, and of John Donne's roving hands going "before, behind, between, above, below." We began to write crisp sentences like W.H. Auden and Graham Greene and used them to discuss Shakespeare and Milton. Jean-Paul Sartre turned us into existentialists, George Orwell into political thinkers, Virginia Woolf into essayists, Leonard Cohen into poets. They were heady years when imagination was electric and words incarnate. By 1965 when I opened Marie-Claire Blais's *Une saison dans la vie d'Emmanuel* and read "Grand-mère Antoinette's feet dominated the room," I didn't need Edmund Wilson to tell me how brilliant the novel was. He never said so in *O Canada*, where he made Blais famous, but that line remains one of the most evocative openings in modern fiction. I handed the book across the table to John Cook, who was reading Leonard Cohen's *The Spice-Box of Earth* and writing almost equally good poetry. He passed it to Arnie Keller, who soon won a Woodrow Wilson fellowship, he to Ariella Blum-Levavi, who had spent her early years in Bergen-Belsen and became a famous speech therapist for the hearing-impaired, and she to Marion Wagschal, a sophisticated reader and already a fine painter.

Fifty years on, those of us still in the city sat together in a Decarie Boulevard funeral parlour staring at the wooden box that held the ashes of our favourite professor, Audrey Bruné. She had arranged the gathering and chosen the pieces we were handed to read. They were all biblical. Mine was a one-liner from St John. Others were longer and each made Audrey's point to its reader. She was religious in her own way. Not a Catholic, she had befriended the two priests who nevertheless did the honours. College teacher Mara Grey cried a little as she read a poem she'd written for the occasion. Teacher and film critic Gordon Peffer found his passage inappropriate. Someone else grumbled at the length of his. The priests played "I know that my redeemer liveth" and we began to share memories of our Stanley Street years.

We may have been McGill rejects but our professors knew possibility. Audrey had a certain rigour to see what was there to be seen. She was enthusiastic to a fault, although not uncritical. She made shy students shine and got permission for women to go where the law prohibited. At ten in the morning she would lead us in her broad-brimmed hat into the Stanley Tavern to hear Sid Lamb deliver his brilliant Shakespeare lectures striding up and down the bar as if he were on the Globe stage. What did he think of us after his years at Cambridge? Betty McLean kindled our love for Milton's *Paradise Lost*, then quoted reams of Wordsworth by heart, wedding our intellects to the goodly universe. From his wheelchair Neil Compton mused on Jonathan Swift and Alexander Pope and taught us how the mind can conquer the body. Wynne Francis brought Sid Lamb's old friend Mordecai Richler to meet us. He had been a student at Sir George in 1950 before leaving for Paris because college had nothing to teach him. He embarrassed her by answering our questions with a flat yes or no. She had Irving Layton read our essays about his poetry and come to tell us why he disagreed, then walk us up to the Carmen to drink with Leonard Cohen when he was there, and to lure anyone willing into his bed.

But it was Audrey who gave us the British and European moderns. She appreciated metaphor beyond historical time. She left us with huge gaps in our literary education but also more curious, more sympathetic, our consciences richer. Perhaps that's why we were closer to her. I reminded the others of the night we watched her waltz with our philosophy professor in the Faculty Club. He was much shorter than she and his head was snuggled between her ample breasts, his eyes closed in ecstasy as they circled the room. We agreed she'd been right to gather us before the priests scattered her ashes above Lake Memphremagog at the Abbaye Saint Benoît. Remembering her reminded us of our younger selves when we talked about nothing but literature and believed her when she told us that we wrote like gods.

For me Stanley Street held another larger blessing. Late one afternoon in mid-September 1964, when I was walking toward the Carmen, I saw Alan Adamson ten yards ahead. He was turned out in a dark grey three-piece suit, blue button-down shirt, and blue and red striped tie. I fell back. When I was thirteen he used to stand on the corner of Westmount Boulevard and Ramezay Road in the morning waiting for a ride to work. He lived in the first of the three old buildings that made up St George's School with his second wife, Leslie, who was one of the teachers. To get there I had to pass him and he terrified me by commenting on my socks. Their colour was the only variation our uniform allowed. And here he was again. I was twenty-three, finishing my Bachelor's degree and working as the college nurse to pay for it. He was forty-five, a newly minted PhD just hired by the History Department. The next day we went to the Tokay for coffee and sat all afternoon talking and falling in love. The physical attraction between us was strong, although we didn't admit it to each other for over a year. It remained through our long marriage. But what I miss most since he died is the conversation that filled our lives.

⁂

Alan had been in Prague for three years from late 1948 learning Czech and teaching English at Charles University's Institute of Modern Languages. He was a socialist, I suppose what we would call a social democrat today, and he was an enquiring historian. Going there at the beginning of the Cold War was foolhardy. So was hastily marrying Leslie Florence, who insisted on accompanying him. As soon as he got on the boat to Europe he realized he had made a dreadful mistake. And worse was to come. When he returned to Montreal in early 1952, the RCMP told him his name was on the McCarthy list. He was not allowed to leave the city and was barred from working as a teacher and in any public institution. He later received a letter from Washington saying that if he entered the United States he'd be arrested.

He had grown up in Winnipeg in a large happy family of professionals with a history traceable to Scotland in the sixteenth century. The family had immigrated to Ireland in the seventeenth century, and to Western Canada in the nineteenth. An Irish relative had married Charlotte Brontë. In the Canadian family there was a head of the Manitoba Court of Appeal nicknamed Hanging Jack, who had once told two brothers acquitted of murder in his court that they were free to go but not to do it again. There were other lawyers, a couple of distinguished doctors, and several notable athletes. Alan's father had been a Rhodes Scholar, his paternal grandfather a Liberal MP. Along with his best friends Ernest Sirluck, George Ford, Stanley Jackson, Frank Pickersgill, and Margaret Ann Bjornson, Alan had belonged to an intellectual group of students at the University of Manitoba called the Morons, who were more equivalent to the Apostles of Cambridge than to my gang of friends, but not unlike us in our devotion to literature. They were among Roy Daniells's first honours students and they often met at his flat to read papers to each other and argue all night. Ernest and George had gone on to become notable literary scholars and university administrators, Stanley to make films with

Norman McLaren at the National Film Board, and Frank to be decorated as a war hero. He was executed in Buchenwald. Alan and Margaret Ann had married and moved to Ottawa to work at the recently founded NFB, he as executive assistant to the commissioner, John Grierson. Margaret Ann was soon posted to New York. They divorced and she eventually married the British filmmaker Sir Arthur Elton.

It was wartime. Alan stayed with Grierson until 1944 but tried twice to enlist and was twice rejected. A mild case of polio had slightly reduced his left calf muscle. On third try it went unnoticed but, before he could complete boot camp, Grierson pulled him out to make combat training films in the far northwest. The army temporarily promoted him to the rank of colonel so that he could move the troops for filming. By the time he finished that assignment, the war was almost over. He used his leg to get himself quickly demobbed, taught briefly at the Workers' Education Association in Toronto, and then directed the Voters' Research Institute in New York and San Francisco before going to Czechoslovakia.

Did his connection with John Grierson contribute to his blacklisting when he returned to Canada? In 1945, when the Soviet cypher clerk Igor Gouzenko defected, he turned over documents proving there was a spy ring operating out of the Russian embassy in Ottawa. Among those mentioned was Freda Linton, one of Grierson's secretaries at the film board. Grierson was not involved and had left the board by then to set up a documentary film business in New York. But the suspicion that surrounded the affair permanently damaged his career and those of several other filmmakers, some of whom, like Alan, became Canadian victims of the McCarran Internal Security Act.

What this meant for Alan was that he had to spend the next seven years selling industrial tools, a job given to him by a friend who also arranged for Leslie to be hired as a secretary at St George's School, then as a teacher. It was not until 1959 when the Gouzenko scare was beginning to be forgotten that he dared to go any distance from the city. He took a job as an instructor in history at the Saskatoon Teachers' College where, according to his painter friend Alfred Pinsky, they were having trouble finding someone to teach Darwin and evolution to their largely Mennonite students. Only in 1961 was he able to get a visa to go to London where he did his PhD with Eric Hobsbawm at Birkbeck College. He was by then forty-two.

During his first year at Sir George, Alan spent a lot of time with me and my friends in the Stanley Street coffee houses, mostly with me talking about literature, his first love, and jazz, about which I then knew little. His marriage had always been unhappy. He and Leslie had separated several times and she had finally agreed to a divorce and to staying in London where she had friends, a flat, and a job. But by Christmas 1964 she had returned to Montreal. And I was engaged to Peter, whose family I had been part of for years, as he had been of mine.

I graduated. May came, and my wedding. I didn't know how to get out of it. My mother was relieved that I was finally getting married, even if not in a church. There was no civil marriage in Quebec in those days and Peter's parents insisted on the synagogue. As we went up the side steps of Temple Emmanuel on Sherbrooke Street to Rabbi Stern's study where a chuppah had been set up, my father chuckled that the marriage might have to be delayed an hour – the Saturday sun had not yet set. Alan and my friends were there. Later at the Mount Stephen Club we ate pheasant and drank champagne. Peter and I were going to Europe for the summer to sleep in a tent and drive nine thousand miles in a red Renault I had paid for by nursing at the Royal Vic in the summers and on weekends. Alan was going to Mexico to write about the peasant revolutionary Emiliano Zapata. When I left he kissed me on the lips for the first time, and long. Also unnoticed by everyone, he slipped his Mexican telephone number into the front of my dress and whispered, "If it doesn't work out, call me."

By November I knew there had to be more to marriage than what was between Peter and me. We separated a few months later, and Alan and I began to live together. There was still no divorce in Quebec and proceedings took their very slow time through the Senate in Ottawa, after which an Act of Parliament dissolved the marriage. Adultery was the only admissible cause. If anything was found amiss in the gathered and usually faked evidence, the case was permanently dismissed. We so much wanted a child that we decided not to wait for divorces that might never be granted. Eventually both decrees came through and we were able to marry six months before Nicholas was born in June 1969. I was then teaching Québécois literature at Loyola College and at the end of term it was not Grand-mère Antoinette's feet that dominated the room during my eleven o'clock lectures but Nicholas's kicking against my dress to the great amusement of my students. For months after he was born, Alan danced about with him, singing Fats Waller's "Don't want you 'cause your feet's too big" and brought friends home to show them off.

2

Graham Greene
No Tape Recorder

In the mid-fifties Montreal was a conservative wasteland for white middle-class teenagers. It still had a racy underbelly but most of the gambling and whorehouses that had made it famous in my Rosemount years had been closed by agreement between the notoriously corrupt Duplessis government and the Catholic Church. We were too young for the downtown nightclubs anyway, although we might have tried to see the legendary stripper Lili St Cyr had she still been around, and we knew nothing of the city's lively jazz scene in Saint-Henri. Sometimes our teachers took us to Her Majesty's Theatre on Guy Street. We heard Pete Seeger get a stuffy audience to sing along quietly with him one evening and we saw several Shakespeare plays there on tour from London. But by the mid-fifties fewer companies stopped in Montreal on their way to Toronto, and in 1963 Her Majesty's was demolished for a parking lot.

Women couldn't sign for their own surgeries or register a child's birth alone. Those of us under sixteen weren't even allowed into the cinema except for the occasional children's film, although we teenage girls had an advantage in our mothers' high-heels and lipstick. So on a winter evening when we headed downtown in search of amusement we usually walked around until we got cold then headed to Ben's Deli on the corner of Mansfield and Burnside for a Coke, or to the only place other than Central Station that didn't throw us out – Classics Bookstore on Sainte-Catherine. The owner, Louis Melzack, used to take our allowances and in return give us what he thought we should read. One Friday in 1955 he handed me a signed copy of Graham Greene's *The Quiet American.* Today it seems a strange match for a fourteen-year-old and I'm not sure it was the book so much as the signature that appealed to me. Louis said it would one day be valuable.

It certainly came in useful the year before Nicholas was born when I walked into the office of Philip Stratford, my assigned PhD director at the Université de Montréal. I wanted to work on Milton. As Phil had just published a monograph about Greene, I mentioned my signed first edition of *The Quiet American.* He smiled and asked, "Do you want to write a thesis or a book?" I didn't know I had a choice but book was obviously the correct answer because it drew a relieved sigh and the suggestion that I tackle Greene's work for the cinema since no one then knew anything about it. I had read *The Power and the Glory* with Audrey Bruné but nothing else of Greene's except *The Quiet American*, and I was teaching Canadian Literature at Loyola College. We talked. Alan had a leave coming up and we were going to London so he could finish writing *Sugar Without Slaves*, a book about the sugar economy in British Guyana after slavery. Phil said that the Greene research would best be done in the British Library and in the circumstances I could do it before finishing my course work. So luck rather than Milton sealed my fate. It found me a very unexpected and publishable subject and a flexible director whose only demand was that I use my scholarly skills to write for ordinary readers. Phil had tracked Greene down when he was himself a graduate student and they had become friends. In those days Graham gave few interviews but he said he would see me in Antibes in October 1970 if Phil came too – and if I did not bring a tape recorder.

The old Library in the British Museum was a room of one's own to generations of literary workers. And so it became to me for many decades, as it did for Alan, who showed me how to use it. From the day I first stood under that great dome, which vaulted up 106 feet and was 140 feet across, 28 feet wider than Wren's at St Paul's, I knew heaven had opened its arms. The galleries around its periphery held some twenty thousand reference books and thousands more were stacked right to its cornice. Above them in the dome itself were twenty great arched windows set between an equal number of gilded, cast-iron ribs. And like a halo above it all, architect Robert Smirke had raised a magnificent glass lantern 40 feet in diameter.

Yet, for all its loftiness, the room was surprisingly cosy, which that late June day I attributed to the gentle summer light falling from its windows and the smell of a century and a half of people and their books. I soon realized the genius of its intimacy was less tonal and more tenacious. But I understood this fully only years later when I was editing Leonard Woolf and Trekkie Ritchie Parsons's correspondence and was brought by mistake the letters Virginia Woolf had left Leonard and her sister, Vanessa, on the mantel at Monk's House before she walked into the River Ouse. Why or how these letters came to me in the Reading Room when they were unordered and should never have left the Manuscript Room remains a mystery. To encounter them so unexpectedly was a physical shock, like stepping on a dead bird in the woods. In that second I knew the dome's secret, its deep privacy and potence.

That Woolf had read there as had many famous writers added to its patina. So did the stories of keepers who checked the waste bins at the end of each day for discarded drafts of future literary treasures and of the semi-feral cats roaming the unseen stacks of books. The room was not quiet. There were elderly scholars who snored gently through the morning, adding to the muted noise of the wooden barrows being pushed up and down the aisles to deliver books and the smack of the heavy green catalogues as they were hoisted to the top of their storage shelves at the centre of the room. Readers coughed and sneezed and whispered audibly as they handed in their requests and searched for someone to take for coffee or, as the day lengthened, to the Museum Tavern across Great Russell Street to liquify their rhetoric. Yet all human sound seemed to rise as inscrutably through the air vents in the lantern as did the smells of old paper, damp coats, and farts. But there was no modern noise in the room, no digital equipment of any kind.

Without computers and with a cumbersome catalogue system that was updated as often as not by hand and frequently out of alphabetical order, you were your own search engine. What you found in your slow human time was not always what you were looking for. And that was part of the richness of your research. You found so much more. The pleasure was in the expansive process of discovery. And in sharing it with other readers who believed that critical discussion and controversy mattered.

That summer Alan sat on my left as I read my way through Graham's then uncollected film criticism and brushed up on the 1930s. To my right sat an old woman who read history and took copious notes. She noticed *Film Form* and *Film Sense* on my desk and the next day gave me a photo of herself standing on a ship with Sergei Eisenstein and his cameraman Dziga Vertov. Her name was Mina Schoeneman Carney. She was an American sculptor whose work I later saw in Dublin's Hugh Lane Gallery. She and her Irish journalist husband, Jack, had been close friends of the famous union organizer Jim Larkin. She had known James Joyce, G.B. Shaw, and Oscar Kokoschka, with whom she had studied in her youth and whose paintings adorned the walls of her small flat in Clifford's Inn. Under her bed were boxes of letters from Joyce, Yeats, and Clarence Darrow. She often joined Alan and me for lunch and sometimes for supper, when she told us about her life and friends.

⚬⚬⚬

In the summer of 1970 Alan left the library early most afternoons to rescue Nicholas from his babysitter while I interviewed film people, the Boulting brothers and Carol Reed among them. Courtesy of the British Film Institute I read many of Graham's scripts and watched all his films in a private screening room. We lived on East Heath Road in Hampstead just where Well Walk crosses it to the Heath. When I got home we'd ramble there and have picnic suppers looking over the city. Before summer was out Nicholas had learned to walk and curled up his toes in objection when we had to put his feet into shoes.

The flat belonged to the Magnum photographer Ian Berry and his journalist wife, Renata, who was about to join him with their two small children on safari in Africa where he was shooting pictures. As the months passed, a man sometimes stood under the streetlight on Well Walk looking up at our windows. The impresario Peter Burman and his pianist wife, Tigger, who lived below, told us he was Renata's friend. She rang just before our lease ended to say we could stay longer if we wanted. She had decided not to return until spring. Had anyone asked about her? The next time Alan saw the poor fellow smoking under the light, he took him to the pub and gave him several whiskies.

It was the best of places to be in London. We'd had a dreadful trip over in early May on the *Empress of Canada*, the trunk of our car stuffed with papers and clothes. Mid-Atlantic, when everyone else was seasick, a diverticulum ruptured in Alan's gut and only the skill of the ship's two Liverpool nurses kept him alive with morphine and their lucky combination of antibiotics. The captain sped the ship to its maximum and arranged to drop us off in Cobh, the port of Cork. The ship's doctor told me Alan would die; the nurses did their best to keep him away from their patient. Alan's fever rose under his delirium and sometime unconsciousness. People knocked from wall to wall going down the halls. At every corner little Nicholas reached out his hand for his Dada, his tears running.

Very early on a still morning three days later, a tender came five miles out from Cobh to fetch us. A door in the ship's hull opened at water level and a couple of wooden planks were placed from it across the ten or so feet of sea to the small boat. Two customs men came aboard, a doctor and a nurse. Alan was taken on a canvas stretcher and placed on a catafalque over the tender's engine. One suitcase went, and Nicholas's teddy bear, Coco. Then, terrified and under strict instruction not to look down, I walked the planks carrying the baby. As soon as I was across the boards were pulled back, the ship's door closed, and we moved quickly away. When I turned around I saw hundreds of passengers watching us from the deck, the ship lopsided with their weight. It continued on to Liverpool. And we were alone on the calm and silent sea for a good half hour before Ireland rose like its metaphorical emerald from the horizon.

An ambulance took us over the cobblestones to Cork with a nurse shouting to the driver to slow down or he'd kill the professor. And then we were in Mercy Hospital and the very skilled hands of Sister Loretta, whose first words to Alan were, "Professor, are you passing wind downward?" With his usual wit he replied weakly, "Yes, sister, that's about all I am doing," and she in her mellow Irish brogue responded, "Ah, you rascal, we'll have you out of here in no time." They laid on hands in that quiet place and healed him. Their x-ray equipment was primitive, the resulting picture inconclusive. But the care was the very best combination of compassion and intelligence, of the art and science of medicine.

As soon as the doctors said Alan was on the mend I flew to Liverpool, picked up the car and luggage from the Canadian Pacific agent, who helped me rope my child-carrying knapsack into the front seat for Nicholas, and drove without a map down the "M" road to London. The baby seemed cognizant of the situation. There was no crying on that very long day until we reached the outer rings of the capital about eight in the evening, and on one of our petrol and nappy-changing stops, when I got him some ice cream, he grabbed the spoon from me with authority and thereafter fed himself. We got almost to Hyde Park Corner before he began to cry continuously and I to feel seriously lost. I hailed a cab to follow to the apartment-hotel in nearby

Elgin Crescent which Alan had booked for us from Montreal. Then, late as it was, I contacted a Canadian acquaintance on sabbatical in London to ask if he had any influential British friends who knew an excellent doctor. I needed to find one quickly so Alan could be transferred from Cork. Pretty soon a Mr Blackburn rang to say Alan's symptoms were those of gall stones and that he would take out his gall bladder at Guy's Hospital. "Tell them in Cork," he said. "They know me." Cork listened and changed their minds about Alan's readiness to fly.

Next morning Nicholas had a high fever and the medicine I was given at the local hospital did nothing to alleviate it. In desperation at the end of another day, I rang 999 for a doctor. "Madame," came the reply. "You need Scotland Yard." Within half an hour an Irishman named Dr Shanahan appeared at the door. He said Nicholas had mononucleosis. A rash would appear next day; the fever would drop and he'd be fine. The medicine I'd been given "rotted the bones of children and pregnant women." And what was I doing in London alone with "a wee babe"?

When Dr Shanahan heard who I'd engaged for Alan he mumbled, "Don't like him. Don't like him." Was his dislike personal or professional? "Professional," he replied. "It's too bad your husband's not a professor." Within another half hour he had arranged for Alan to be treated by the University of London's professor of surgery at the Lindo Wing of St Mary's Hospital, Paddington.

In Cork there was relief. They said that Mr Blackburn had botched Anthony Eden's gall bladder operation and Eden had quietly had it repaired in New York. The Cork doctors had decided to keep Alan in Ireland until he was well but would now put him on a plane. I was hugely relieved too. I took Nicholas for a long walk in the spring air. When I got back Ariella Blum-Levavi and her husband, Jules Samson, were sitting on the doorstep. They had heard what happened from my mother and without telling anyone had generously come to take care of the baby. Next morning I met Alan at Heathrow with a wheelchair and took him to St Mary's, where he recuperated for another week. No gall bladder problem. The ruptured diverticulum that the Cork doctors couldn't image clearly they had diagnosed correctly and cured without surgery.

When the baby saw Alan he threw himself from my arms into his father's. On his face was an adult's understanding of loss and redemption. Neither of us ever forgot that look. Some family stories are told so often they become almost public legend. This one was repeated in two voices to everyone's amusement for decades. Alan always thought the effect on Nicholas must have been tremendous. And perhaps it was. But, with no memory of what happened, his knowledge of it is fictional, public, and jovial. It's now one of his own ghost stories, along with that of Alan slipping his Mexican phone number into my dress at the top of the great staircase in the Mount Stephen Club and me ringing him when things didn't work out. Somewhere in an Irish archive there's a front-page Cork newspaper photo of us rising up the perpendicular iron ladder to the Cobh dock from the tender below – Alan on his stretcher at a precarious angle, Coco Bear being handed up, then Nicholas, then me.

○ ○ ○

The great day came. When we drove into Antibes on 27 October 1970 and pulled up at a stoplight, Alan told me to look left. There beside us sat a shrunken Picasso in his white Cadillac. Phil Stratford was on sabbatical with his wife and many children in a rented villa in nearby Juan les Pins. As he and I stood outside Graham's flat on Avenue Pasteur the next day, Phil promised to stay completely out of the interview. But he warned me to be careful because Graham was addicted to practical jokes.

The flat was small and curiously impersonal. In the living room a writing table with its papers and notebooks neatly piled along one side was placed beside a wall of windows. Outside was a stretch of balcony and a view of the marina. An adjoining wall had bookshelves that seemed to hold fewer books than small empty whisky bottles. Yvonne Cloetta, Graham's de facto wife, was already there. Immediately Graham insisted we have a martini. That he handed me the largest of the four juice glasses filled to the brim and without the benefit of ice should have put me on the alert. But I was nervous and trying so hard to be sophisticated that I took the inequity as politeness on his part, thinking I would have a few sips and leave the rest.

Graham placed me in a chair against the inner wall and Phil well away from me on the sofa beside Yvonne. Above them hung a small painting by Cuban artist René Portocarrero that Castro had given him. He said he wasn't sure he'd hung it right way up because the signature was on the reverse and he couldn't tell which was the top. He sat himself across from me with his back to the window, the midday Mediterranean sun streaming past him straight into my eyes. We began to talk. Very soon his gentle suggestions made me understand that there would be no lunch until I finished my entire drink. When I eyed the enormous plant beside my chair with every intention of feeding it four ounces of the driest and warmest martini I've ever tasted, Graham allowed that he had potted the avocado himself. But he never removed his pale blue eyes from my glass, even as he refilled everyone else's. Years later he told me he had lied about planting the avocado.

I somehow downed the martini and we went to lunch at a small restaurant in Valbonne above Antibes which Phil claimed to have cased in preparation for the interview. Graham ordered the wine. We were by then only three. Three bottles appeared, and we settled into a lengthy French meal. At the time, Graham's engagement with the cinema went back some forty years and thanks to my months in the Reading Room I knew more about it than he remembered. Good to his promise, Phil kept to his wine while Graham and I chatted amiably about his films, the 1930s, his years reviewing cinema for *The Spectator* and the ill-fated *Night and Day*, in which he wrote on 28 October 1937 that Shirley Temple had ostensibly wiggled her bottom across the screen in *Wee Willie Winkie* to the delight of the old men in the back row. She was nine. She and 20th Century Fox jointly sued him and closed down the magazine, while he fled to Mexico to report on religious persecution and avoid having to appear in court. "Yes," he said, "my solicitor told me to get out of England to avoid the dock. I hated Mexico."

Everything went well until Phil left the table for a few moments and returned with the pained disclosure that the restaurant had no toilet. I thought that more a problem for me than for him since this was France and there were several leafy corners in the parking lot. Graham's superior bladder evidently rendered the situation entirely academic. He ordered another bottle of wine and sank back into the 1930s while I learned that the only advantage of extreme physical discomfort is that it keeps you alert.

Perhaps that's why he remembered me. He liked raw stamina. And he liked women whose beauty went before them, its recognition taken for granted. When we parted that evening I had no reason to expect that I would ever see him again. In the spring of 1972 I published an article about his film criticism in *Sight and Sound* and sent him a copy. He wrote back thanking me, and when I had questions about his film work we corresponded again.

Then on 26 March 1979 Penelope Gilliatt lifted the meat of "Graham Greene as Film Critic" for her *New Yorker* "Profile" without a syllable of acknowledgment. Graham came to my rescue along with Penelope Houston, then editor of *Sight and Sound.* Gilliatt had also copied writer Michael Mewshaw in her article and made enormous errors of her own invention. I wanted a printed apology but, while *New Yorker* editor William Shawn acknowledged the "shocking similarities" on the phone on 3 May, he made it clear he would not print one. Gilliatt, he said, was "very sick" and I "must be compassionate." He would do everything in his power to keep the issue quiet because *The New Yorker* had been sued for saying in its 27 February issue that the famous fish restaurant Lutèce had served frozen turbot. I later learned in Renata

Adler's memoir, *Gone: The Last Days of The New Yorker* (1999), that Shawn had known for some time about Gilliatt's plagiarism and done nothing. Also that he played me against Mewshaw.

My lawyer was told by the magazine's lawyer that I would certainly win the case but that they'd make sure it would take long and expensive years to get it through the courts. I took the thousand American dollars they offered and refused to sign a paper saying I would keep quiet. It turned out that Mewshaw was paid twice that, the extra thousand to forgo the acknowledgment I had also asked for. Shawn fired Gilliatt under the guise of sick leave, the real reason vanishing into New York gossip. I tried many times without success to get the details into print but only succeeded when Mewshaw reviewed Shirley Hazzard's *Greene on Capri* for the *Los Angeles Times* on 6 February 2000. A 12 March letter to the Books Editor telling my part of the story did the trick, finally putting the two pieces together.

Of course these days far worse happens all the time but what Shawn allowed Gilliatt to get away with was not unconscious plagiarism as he told Mewshaw. It was theft. And his promise to both Mewshaw and myself never to republish the "Profile" was not kept. Gilliatt's piece is now part of *The New Yorker on CD*, where evidently paper copyright does not hold. The affair gave me a strong negative appreciation of the power of the commercial press and a distrust of journalists equal to Graham's, who insisted on being called a reporter when he travelled the world to write political articles.

After that first meeting Graham usually told me to pour my own drinks, which I took to mean that he never forgot my trial by martini. He was a prankster, no question. He entered literary competitions under fake names. He and film producer John Sutro founded the Anglo-Texan Society as a joke in 1953 and got the American Air Force to provide twenty-eight hundred pounds of prime US beef for a party they gave at Denham Studios. I once saw a brass plaque marking this occasion somewhere east of the Strand but was never able to find it again. Perhaps Graham had it taken down after I told him I'd seen it, just as he wanted a couple of his early books destroyed when he decided they weren't to his credit. Then there was the invention of a Mrs Montgomery who created havoc at Eyre and Spottiswoode for months in the fifties by claiming the press had lost her manuscript. The list is very long.

For me it was other trials. Early on, and when he knew it was marketable, Graham told me he had edited Charlie Chaplin's autobiography, cutting from it thousands of words. I was not to publish this. I didn't until I wrote the biography of his publisher, Max Reinhardt, after Graham died and had the papers in hand to prove its truth. Graham waited a few months to make sure I kept mum. Then came other disclosures, sometimes with the same directive. In July 1988, two months after Kim Philby died in May, and when he and Yvonne were planning to return to Russia where he was given an honorary doctorate by the University of Moscow and an eighty-eighth birthday party by the Writers' Union, he proposed some political mischief by making me promise to send him a provocative telegram which he would write. This prank he aborted. Or perhaps he found a more direct route by interrupting a birthday toast to him with one of his own to "the wife of my close friend who died not long ago and to whom I was bound by warm memories."

I never knew what he had up his sleeve but I'm sure the Chaplin business was to test my integrity more than it was to amuse. Loyalty was important to Graham. He controlled his career as tightly as he did a sentence. He said his desire to be successful came from a sense of inferiority and wrote in many places about his confused boyhood loyalties as he passed through the green baize door from home to school where Charles Greene changed from father to headmaster. What I became only recently aware of was the huge number of old boys from Berkhamsted School who had died in the First World War. Of the 1,145 who enlisted, 184 died and 177 were wounded. In 1934 in *The Old School* Graham wrote about his generation being betrayed by their old men. But he never mentioned how he felt watching his father add the names of those young men to the death roster, many of whom were almost like sons to Charles Greene. Only that his generation would better their fathers'. Was this in part the source of his ambition?

He was rightly concerned with the production of his own books, and with Max Reinhardt at The Bodley Head and then at Reinhardt Books he achieved the kind of publishing control few modern novelists had, other than perhaps Virginia Woolf. But even as he achieved that partnership, Graham tried to move himself into a position at Heinemann that would have given him more profitable control of his work. Against Max's better judgment he pulled his friend into the deal and, when it failed, publicly blamed A.S. Frere, an older friend and his long-time publisher before Max. Graham had many financial responsibilities and counted on his pen to fulfil them. When I met him it was unusual for him to give interviews. He continued to judiciously and profitably control his public image.

"No tape recorder" was that first afternoon's condition. What I didn't know then was that Graham's rule was more to my benefit than to his. Not recording interviews became my biographer's practice. It made everyone talk more freely and me listen more carefully and remember better not just what was said and how but what people wore, what they did with their hands, what was on their walls and outside their windows. Agatha Christie advised writers starting out on a career in detective fiction to be careful in creating a central character because they might have to live with that person for a long time. I soon learned that writing biography means you are similarly subsumed for years in someone else's life, visiting archives, taking notes, writing letters, hunting people down and interviewing as many of them as you can. And this is just the getting of facts. You then have to set them down with the care and attention of a historian and novelist combined. And you have to be careful. People talk because they want you to write their story, but you have a responsibility to them in what you put down. Without a tape recorder a watchfulness was added to my conversations as time shifted from memory to storytelling to biographical narrative.

I always checked with people before publication and what I remembered was never challenged. However provident Graham's directive was, I found this strange since memory is selective and confected. But perhaps that's more true for novelists. Repetition, however reconstructed, certainly gives memory flesh.

In 1982 during Graham's confrontation with the Mafia on behalf of Yvonne's daughter Martine, which occasioned his *J'Accuse: The Dark Side of Nice*, I was told by his sister Elisabeth to ring him as soon as I got to Antibes. He was worried about me, she said. The police answered the phone. They told me to hang up and ring again. Graham answered. Being careful, I said nothing about this until we were face to face next morning. He claimed not to know the police were monitoring his calls. I believed him. Then he said someone had tried to break his door down. Of this I saw no evidence. He said he was being watched and, standing behind me, made me look down to the marina through curtains I'd never seen closed before. Was anyone looking up from there? Not that I could see. Then he said he'd acquired a gun. Did I think that wise? He looked me straight in the eye at close distance long enough for me to know we were both remembering the story of his late-teenage games of Russian roulette. He was frightened. Very frightened. Was he also dramatizing a memory I knew was not exact when he added it to his record? I don't know. His nephew Nick Dennys told me that he'd been in Antibes only a few days before I had and that Graham had asked him too if he should get a gun. Nick had said it was too dangerous, that Graham was safe because the Mafia would not want it known that they'd killed a famous writer. Had he got one after all? Nick thought not. But sometimes relatives get it plain wrong.

Graham never interfered with what I wrote about him but he was always happy when I sent him an article in advance of publication. On those occasions he seemed admirably detached and genuinely interested in himself as a figure in my imagination. Sometimes he even unconsciously appropriated my interpretation of him. Early on he began quoting verbatim what I had written about techniques I thought he'd learned from the hundreds of films he'd watched as a cinema critic. When I suggested that what he was saying was in my manuscript on his writing table he said, "Oh yes, yes," and continued to quote me. He had previously insisted his writing was not cinematic but thereafter told everyone about the influence of film on his novels. This is now common currency. Did my research override his memory or was it simply added to his advantage? On 21 June 1982 I reminded him about a script for *The Tenth Man* that he had written for MGM. I had told him in 1970 when I found it in the Humanities Research Library in Texas where most of his early papers are held. In 1970 he said that it might date back to before the war. In 1982 he said he had forgotten that I'd told him about it before. A few months later he alerted the press with an unlikely but typical Graham story about finding the script in a box in a storage cupboard when he was looking for a tennis racquet. By April 1984 that story had been spun into publicity for the book and film.

He hated to talk about his own work. Once finished he lost interest in his novels apart from commercial concerns, and he tossed off critical consideration with, "It's all unconscious you know." He frequently confused the names of his characters and once a book had been screened he said he had difficulty reimagining his own protagonists. But he showed a keen interest in my scholarly work. Perhaps it suggested his hunt for material. Soon after I met him he offered to disguise himself and come to Texas to smuggle out his own letters. On another occasion he asked if he could help me in a less well-guarded archive. He certainly liked the smell and feel of old books and paper. But here again pleasure was mixed with business. He advised even his mistresses to sell off his letters to them.

When we began *Reflections* I was writing *The Dangerous Edge* (1990) and had just published "Looking for the Third Man" in *Encounter* (June 1978) and *Der Monat (Febr/März 1979)* jointly with Phil. That was the first article to outline the many differences between the film and its treatment, which surfaced as the story Graham said was never written to be read, along with all the differences between its

British and American editions. It showed the interesting Cold War pattern that affected the film but is rarely mentioned today when the story and film are compared.

As I gathered material for *Reflections* I would send Graham what I found in the archives by the decade. When I came to the sixties I discovered that most of the articles I turned up were in *Ways of Escape* (1980), which had been marketed as autobiography. We had agreed I would use only uncollected material, so with my next batch of xeroxes I sent a careful letter saying I hadn't realized how heavily he'd relied on his journalism for that book. Back came a scathing attack on the quality of the xeroxes which he deemed, incorrectly, to be unreadable. There was nothing about the problem at hand. Only after hours of working with a photographer to correct the losses from copying old newspapers and microfilm did I realize the significance of the way Graham had signed the letter. Above his name he had written, "I'm sorry."

I saw this self-protective anger again one morning in Antibes. We'd been talking for a couple of hours when the telephone rang. Graham went into the hall to answer it and what I overheard went something like this: "No, I don't want to do that, thank you." Silence. "No, I don't want to do that." Silence. "I told you no in my letter. Now please leave me alone." – "I've said no. I'm busy now." – "No, don't phone me back. Just leave me alone." – "Why can't you leave me alone?" Bang. He returned to the living room shaking. It was an Italian woman who wanted him to put some photos he'd taken into an exhibition she was mounting. He was inconsolable. Even the double martini I made for him was powerless against his entangled anger, guilt, and resentment. The woman had got the better of him and he was deeply humiliated.

Yvonne came soon to take us to Felix's in the port for lunch and she held him tightly until he calmed down. At the restaurant he was as eager as ever for a bit of gossip. When he began remembering Cunard voyages, I told him about Alan's hair-raising experience on the Atlantic. It was late afternoon and I made a serious effort to shorten the long story. But at every stop Graham repeated my last words and prodded me almost like a child, "And then? And then?" He'd always been frighteningly quick at editorial decisions. I once handed him an article he hadn't seen for forty years and watched him pen corrections three paragraphs down as soon as he took it from me. And I'd seen his absorption of my work as his own. But I'd never before felt the pull of his writer's imagination extracting detail for future use.

The story over, he asked for the name of the ship. When I answered the *Empress of Canada,* his head drooped and he said almost to himself, "but that isn't a Cunard ship." I hadn't said it was, but I knew instantly that for whatever purpose he wanted the story, I had told it wrong. Into my silent embarrassment he then began an entirely unrelated account of eating with Max Reinhardt and Carol Reed at Anton Karas's wine garden in Vienna. Karas, whose zither music made *The Third Man* so much money, had invited them to come when he opened the place. After a lively evening of drinking and reminiscing he'd had the effrontery to present them with a bill. Max said he'd pay it; Graham was furious and said he must not. He was so angry that he walked out and stamped all the flowers in Karas's garden into the earth and was caught, to his embarrassment, by Max, who came out just as mortified at having paid the bill to avoid a scene. Years later Max told me the same story, laughing at how embarrassed they both had been. Graham sounded no less red-faced then than he had been the first time I'd used the small loo in his flat and he'd so rushed, as he said, "to prepare it" for me that we'd ended up both holding the toilet seat he'd been trying to put down.

He gave me a tight hug at the airport that evening and I returned to London feeling vaguely redeemed, if dumb. I had trespassed on something intimate in the most gifted of storytellers. But what? Where his reporter's truth had sometimes seemed to me as slippery as fine silk, his blighted Cunard hope enshrined his insistence on accurate fictional detail. Both his reputation and his aesthetic sense depended on it. I never figured out what had so intrigued him in my story that it could not have happened on a Cunard ship, except that it lacked Cunard's famed association with champagne. But I knew that the jump between discernible fact and his novelist's truth was tricky and magical, and that I had unwittingly violated its successful transubstantiation.

The last time I saw Graham was at the end of May 1989. He was already very ill and *Reflections* was well on its way. He was trying to raise his haemoglobin by eating steak tartare, which Yvonne and I both thought unwise. Usually full of intellectual energy and fun, he was now fatigable but she filled in his lapses so seamlessly that if I hadn't known him before I wouldn't have noticed. We spoke on the phone a few times after that day. Then he went to Switzerland and Max Reinhardt called one morning in the early spring of 1990 to say Graham wanted to talk. Would I please ring him?

When he came on the line I asked immediately how he was. "Waiting," he said. It took a few seconds for me to realize his intention. He was waiting for death. He wanted a poem I'd rejected added to *Reflections*, which was already prepared for the printer. I had a cinema article to include that he wanted forgotten. We agreed to add both. Then he said in a quietly worn voice, "Thank you for your introduction. I told Max to tell you it's the best thing in the collection." He had told Phil Stratford the same but I'd forgotten. "Graham, you know that's untrue," I said, "but thank you for saying it." I'm sure he smiled errant as we bid our final goodbyes.

✿✿✿

Westminster Cathedral, Thursday, 6 June 1991, 11 AM.

Graham's family sat on the right, the rest of us on the left. Yvonne was a few rows ahead of me, protected by Graham's publisher, Max Reinhardt, and his wife, Joan. Mrs Graham Greene, as she listed herself in the Oxford telephone directory, sat closer to the front on the opposite side between Graham's son, Francis, and his daughter, Caroline. The procession began with the crucifer's cross followed by five or six priests holding candles and swirling censers, and altar boys in ascending then descending height. The Right Reverend Monsignor Patrick O'Donoghue took up the rear. In the sanctuary the boys were nudged into place by the priests. "Requiem aeternam dona eis, Domine: et lux perpetua luceat eis ..."

When the Communion itself began, the aisles filled with men in morning suits and women in hats, their gloved hands now bare. "Oh, there's Pinkie," I thought, watching Richard Attenborough. As the shuffle thinned, another of Graham's characters appeared. A doddery late-middle-aged woman in a dirty mac and head scarf came up the centre aisle and slipped into the seat beside Caroline. From farther down the pew Graham's grandson, Andrew, mouthed "Who is she?" to his mother, who shrugged as she continued her prayers. Mrs Graham Greene was led to another place by an usher as the choir continued, "Ave verum corpus, natum de Marie Virgine ..."

Then all was quiet and Louise Dennys went to the pulpit. Graham, she said of her uncle, was always loyal to the people he loved, but he never turned up to family weddings, christenings, or funerals. Muriel Spark reminded us that with each £20 monthly cheque Graham had sent to support her early writing there came a few bottles of good red wine to take the edge off cold charity. The last time she'd seen him they'd made up a mystery story called "The Missing OM." There can be only twenty-four members in possession of the Order of Merit at any one time, she explained. Graham had been admitted in 1986. As one had just died when she and Graham met they'd imagined one of the two who might fill the place being murdered by the other contender. It was a promising opening and, Graham now dead, she thought of the missing OM.

Spark was so short her head barely cleared the pulpit. Perhaps that's why the uninvited woman got up as Spark spoke, crossed the aisle from the relatives' side of the cathedral and plonked herself in the empty second row of ours. When Alec Guinness began his tribute she must have recognized him and rose again to sit in the middle of the first pew, directly under the pulpit. As the last priests sent Graham off with their incense and flapping surplices our anonymous woman vanished. Perhaps she exited the side door with Guinness and Spark and slipped into one of their limousines as we earnestly sang "The day thou gavest, Lord, is ended …" Too bad. She might have travelled with Aunt Augusta straight into another story.

3
The Dawson Years

On 16 October 1970, as we were about to leave London for Antibes and that first meeting with Graham, we woke to the BBC announcement that the Canadian Army were in the streets of Montreal. The British trade commissioner, James Cross, had been kidnapped by the Front de libération du Québec on 5 October, and on the 10th, Pierre Laporte, minister of labour and vice-premier of the province. Prime Minister Pierre Trudeau had invoked the War Measures Act at four o'clock that morning. It was a politically risky move in the face of Quebec's increasing awareness of itself as a culture different in many ways from the rest of Canada. Civil rights were suspended. People were rounded up for questioning. On our way to France the next day we heard that Laporte had been murdered and demands sent for the release of Cross.

When we got back to Montreal a few months later, the city was still heavy with political argument. Almost as soon as we arrived we met historian George Rudé and his wife, Doreen. Before we'd gone to London, Eric Hobsbawm had told Alan that George might be interested in joining Sir George Williams's History Department. When he came to be interviewed we'd taken him to breakfast at the Ritz and convinced him of Montreal's charm despite its deep political problems.

We'd also had dinner there with Conor Cruise O'Brien and his wife, Màire, when Conor came to be interviewed. He was elected to the Irish Parliament soon afterward, so the university lost him. But the day we breakfasted with George he was in a sticky situation, having accepted a post at the University of Stirling in Scotland where Doreen refused to live. From her point of view Montreal was the better choice, and we became very close friends. She loved children and embraced Nicholas as her own. Having had a successful life as a broadcaster in Australia where George had taught for several years, she was unhappy at first in Montreal and filled her time by insisting we stop for tea in the afternoon and dress for dinner parties in the evening. At Doreen's table political discussion was still *de rigueur* but its tone was less strident. She appreciated the comedy of political life and gathered our friends into an intellectual gentility in which we were expected to sparkle, not lead the troops.

So our academic life in Montreal began in earnest. Within a few years Alan and I found ourselves in possession of 11 Richelieu Place, which reminded us of London, and where Doreen spent hours at tea time playing old favourites on the piano while whoever else was there bellowed along, and a cottage in Sutton in Quebec's Eastern Townships. There we spent weekends and summers when we didn't return to England, writing and pleasurably cultivating the land like early-Canadian farmers.

✪✪✪

Dawson College was two years old when I began to teach English there in 1971. It was housed in a red brick factory building on Selby Street in Saint-Henri with additional classrooms three blocks further west on du Couvent. Both buildings were run-down and the annex was made of cement blocks that registered above the acceptable level of radiation on a Geiger counter. A heritage building also in need of renovation was soon acquired on Viger Square in the old city, and a couple of years after that a high-rise apartment building close to Lafontaine Park. Other spaces followed, most in equal disrepair, totalling seventeen in all. Finally in 1988 we moved to Sherbrooke Street into the Mother House that had once been home to thousands of nuns in the Congregation of Notre Dame. Our director general, Sarah Paltiel, had got us the building three years earlier by going regularly to Quebec City and waiting on a bench outside the National Assembly for the premier to come out so she could plead our cause face to face. In that extensively renovated historic setting surrounded by fourteen inner-city acres of lawn and trees, we were suddenly the college of choice. Where from 1969 we'd taken in any student who wanted to come, we now attracted so many that even some of the province's best had to be turned away.

My first year at Dawson was sobering. The new compulsory two-year college program fitted into Quebec's revamped education system between four years of high school and a three-year Bachelor's degree. On the English side it was in essence the first year of university divided in two, with many three-year professional programs like mechanical technology and nursing running alongside. After our research year in London I'd spent another year writing my PhD thesis on a Canada Council Doctoral Grant and I returned to the classroom expecting the students to have a certain level of literacy. What I found was that many of them couldn't read well and from my university point of view the English curriculum was disorganized, the idea being that students should study whatever interested them. As English and humanities courses were compulsory for everyone in both years, which was a fine principle, future brain surgeons sat shoulder to shoulder with future car mechanics and plumbers, students from deprived areas of the city with those from private schools.

In the Selby annex on du Couvent Street where I was first posted, I often had to step over students sitting stoned on the hall floor to get to my office. One morning I found a newly hired colleague waiting at the door for me. She'd been teaching in England and against my advice insisted on wearing her academic gown to class. But she wasn't as out of place as I imagined. Her students appreciated what I'm sure they thought was a fancy costume and asked if she wanted a drag on their joint.

Mine were less enterprising, perhaps because many of them were fatigued from working long hours at menial jobs outside school hours. Two I remember from those early years were Ricky and Benny, both first-generation Italians, one tall and thin, the other rotund and short. They seemed to be functionally illiterate in three languages and switched from one to the other in constant spat. One day the taller one picked up the heavier one in his chair, raised it several feet off the floor and let it drop. Neither was hurt but they wouldn't leave the lecture they'd disrupted until I got a guard to throw them out. I was repaid with a bashed office door. My colleagues had bad days like that too, partly caused by the loose ambience of the early seventies but also because so many of our students came from families where no one had finished high school and, while there was encouragement for education, there was little understanding of what it entailed. This was not in every program of course; Adam Gopnik and Steven Pinker were among our early graduates. But there seemed to be more Rickys and Bennys in those first years and they made us inventive teachers.

Once I settled in I found the place exciting. We were creating a new kind of institution and were given almost complete freedom to make things up as we went along. We had a strong sense of Dawson as unique and an equally strong commitment to providing higher education for anyone who wanted it. Our then director general, Paul Gallagher, called us "a community of learners." I would have added of multi-cultural, inner-city learners made up of students with unequal preparation and different expectations and, certainly in my department, a faculty that creatively, if not always successfully, addressed the enormous challenge of inventing a curriculum for them.

Another young man I remember had been admitted to McGill's Law Faculty. He was intelligent and had an attentive memory but he was a very poor reader. He was in his final term at Dawson and had passed his other English courses by memorizing lectures and writing them back on essays and exams, something we soon realized many ambitious first-generation immigrant students also did until they learned the language well enough not to have to. This fellow was reading at a level so low that I knew he wouldn't survive in law school. When I told him so he threw a book at me and swore his way out of my office. He returned a week later to say he knew that reading is more than picking words off the page, which was an intelligent comment if not an apology. We spent many of my holiday hours together that summer and he easily measured up at McGill in September. However, my colleagues who had passed him with high grades never forgave me for pointing out their negligence, which to my mind was a sign of the fundamental problem in the department – how best to teach such varied students.

Like them, we teachers came in all shapes, sizes, and personalities. We were a good mix of scholars, having at the time more PhDs among us than McGill's English Department, several published novelists, poets, and one playwright. We were young and most of us were writing as well as teaching. But since Dawson was positioned between high school and a shortened Bachelor's program, we didn't always agree on what our incoming students should be taught. Those of us who were high school–oriented thought an old-fashioned composition course was the place to begin. Those of us with a university outlook believed that the root of many of our students' problems was their lack of general education, and that we should start with a course that would provide some of the literary and historical knowledge required for good reading, and for critical thinking and writing. As Muriel Spark's Jean Brodie said, education is a leading out of ignorance and insularity.

As the department grew, we continued to argue. To our credit, we never stopped experimenting as we sought solutions, but our curricular disputes became more contentious as the years passed and as the verbal slide between the best and the worst students increased. Finally Yvonne Klein, a prize-winning translator and writer hired a year or two after me, and I convinced our colleagues to let us administer a standard reading test to all new students. The test was found for us by Helen Wehden, a New Yorker who knew more about learning problems and how to help students get over them than anyone at the college, and we created remedial courses for those who needed them. But even a decade after we'd done this the discussion continued, now about what should be taught to those students whose reading levels were sometimes as low as third grade.

✪✪✪

By then we had another problem. In 1974 Quebec's Liberal premier, Robert Bourassa, passed Bill 22, making French the official language of the province and forcing all immigrants into French schools. The following year his government passed the Quebec Charter of Human Rights and Freedoms, which guaranteed freedom of expression – but also to some extent contradicted Bill 22. In 1976 René Lévesque's Parti Québécois government came to power and a year later toughened Bill 22 with Bill 101, the Charter of the French Language.

Then the serious wrangling began. Quebec's French Language charter and its Charter of Human Rights and Freedoms were challenged in Quebec's provincial and Canada's federal courts several times as the government moved from the hands of the Liberals under Bourassa (1970–76 and 1985–94) to those of the Parti Québécois under Lévesque in the intervening years (1976–85). But the question remained: which of the charters took precedence, that of the French language or that guaranteeing freedom of speech?

In 1980, the year of the first referendum on the possible separation of Quebec from Canada, which failed by just under 20 per cent, the Supreme Court of Canada supported a judgment by the Quebec Superior Court striking down the section of Bill 101 that made French the language of the legislature and courts in the province. In 1984 another Supreme Court judgment ruled that Bill 101's ability to stop children who moved to Quebec from other provinces from attending English schools was unconstitutional. As well, and picking up on the contradictory natures of Quebec's charters of Language and of

Human Rights, it ruled that the exclusive use of French on public commercial signs was contrary to freedom of speech. So that provision of Bill 101 requiring that signs appear in French only was also struck down.

In 1988, to prevent another challenge to Bill 101, Bourassa took the extraordinary step of invoking section 33, the notwithstanding clause of Canada's Charter of Rights and Freedoms, and passed Bill 178. It allowed English on interior but not exterior business signs. Then, largely because of the arguments of Claude Ryan, who had led the Liberals between 1978 and 1982, Bill 86 was passed. It allowed English on outside signs as long as the French words were twice the size.

To anyone outside Canada, perhaps even outside Quebec, this may all sound picayune and in part amusing. But the struggle for French dominance was accompanied by a desire for independence and in 1995 a second referendum on separation from Canada was held and failed, this time by less than one per cent. Everyone who lived through those harrowing years watched as one culture altered another.

Most immigrant students already spoke English or wanted to learn it when they came to Quebec. Before 1974 they usually attended English schools and had been integrated into the English community by the time they got to Dawson. This was exactly what Bill 22 was designed to stop. From then on immigrants were only allowed to enter the English system after high school, and their experience in French schools had often been difficult. Even into the 1990s newspapers reported that immigrant children were bullied in class and beaten up in schoolyards, bused to schools away from their neighbourhoods to spread them out, and not allowed to speak English on school property. When the numbers of these French-schooled students increased at Dawson, we had a second-, and in most cases a third-language problem to deal with.

We adjusted by adding more remedial courses. By the mid-eighties they were so abundant that we all had to teach one every year and many of us dreaded them. I did not, and I continued to argue for teaching challenging literature in them and to question the efficacy of courses that did not. Eventually I got the department to allow me a small experiment. I would teach the same survey course of Western literature to two sections of the lowest-ranking incoming students and two groups of the regular first-year students concurrently. I'd test the students at the beginning and end of term and see which group's reading scores rose faster.

At first the teaching was terribly hard in the remedial sections because the reading was difficult. I quizzed the students every class to make sure they kept up. They complained of course, but as the weeks passed they began to understand that looking up words in the dictionary was only the beginning of knowing what they meant, that words belong to a context, books to a cultural tradition. Soon, enough students became excited by what they were reading to stimulate the others. It took every scrap of my knowledge and ingenuity to teach them. One day, in sheer frustration, a fellow shouted out, "What are you teaching us, English or biology?" It was a fair question in a discussion about Andrew Marvell's "To His Coy Mistress." I even added old-fashioned spelling bees to the mix for half an hour every Friday, dividing the students into teams and drilling them on words from their reading which they had to spell, define, and put into a sentence. There was always laughter on Fridays and at term's end I happily bought beer for the winning team, coffee for the losers.

What happened could have been predicted. In the two regular literature classes, reading scores on entry had ranged from eighth grade to second-year-university level; in the remedial groups from third to seventh grade. At the end of the fifteen-week term the reading scores of the regular students had risen by two or three grades, those of the remedial students between six and ten grades, which saw them approximately on an equal footing with the regular students and well prepared for any literature course in their second term. What seemed even better to me, the students poorer on entry now wanted to read; they had begun to understand language as something more than a technical accomplishment, punctuation as a set of rules they could use to regulate their ideas, and essays as interesting and open-ended discussions rather than the five templated paragraphs many of my colleagues were by then teaching.

But my department's years of pedagogical argument had been pernicious in their cumulative effect. Yes, yes, my colleagues said and carried on as though my small experiment had proved nothing. And perhaps it hadn't. By then government intervention in the curriculum had begun in earnest. I think partly in self-defence, more of my colleagues began to teach technical writing and other courses the administration encouraged that were directed to specific professional programs. The cognitive value of literature was being abandoned and a voice in my head kept telling me we were fostering the change.

Then, in 1983, Lévesque's government wanted to roll back the hard-won gains that we'd made in class sizes and numbers of teaching hours during Bourassa's Liberal years. On 26 January we joined a strike of 9,500 college teachers. There soon followed eighty thousand primary and high school teachers, affecting about one and a half million students, then daycare workers with sympathetic parents filling in for them, and some health care workers, with more being added daily to protest their long hospital hours.

Being on strike is a nasty business. I was assigned picket duty at the Viger building in the old city where bitter winter winds howled up from the river. Four of us trudged around that Rococo block of limestone for several hours every night, walking from different corners of it to the middle of the building and back so that we could keep an eye on one another. Economist Voyo Kovalski and novelist Keith Harrison were on the front stretch, another English Department colleague, Hugh Nelson, and I on the back. The nights were long, but not without humour. About three one morning a sinister-looking figure loomed out of the alley across the street. His pace was steady and his direction clear. I was in his sights. Hugh saw him too and ran protectively toward me. In the man's hand as it came out of his bulging right pocket was a pack of cigarettes and two one-dollar bills. "It's cold," the fellow said. "Go buy yourselves some coffee."

Another night Hugh and I were sent with Herman Carter, an American draft dodger who'd been a student of Alan's and was now teaching history at Dawson, and Gus Fagin, a hot-headed Newfoundlander in the Humanities Department, to paste union posters on a wall east of Place des Arts. Hugh and Gus did the first shift while Herman and I stayed in my car. After we changed places the police drove up. There were posters on that wall for pop singers, for Lili Krause, and Les Grands Ballets. Why couldn't we put up some for our union? The police told us to give them the bucket of paste, the brush, and the posters and go home. As we were handing things over, Gus jumped out of the car, grabbed the posters, and shouted, "They belong to my union." So Herman and I were arrested – the Black and the dame.

Hugh took the car home for me. At the station, which was on a deserted street east of Place des Arts, there were about thirty more teachers in a similar position, all from French colleges. Two women were behind bars. A third cell door waited open. We stood at the end of the line headed by three policemen who were filling out papers behind a counter. Herman whispered "they look stoned." An American citizen, he was terrified; his Canadian papers were not yet in order. When it came our turn everyone had gone except the two women in the cells. I told Herman to speak first and moved beside him to flirt with the officers, hoping they would let him go, which they did. At the outer door he looked back more guilty than afraid as the police came toward me from behind the counter. Never was I so happy for a middle-class address. When I said Richelieu Place they backed off, although they followed me to the house, where Alan and Hugh, both political veterans, were inside drinking whisky. Next morning in court Herman and I pleaded *coupable* and were fined.

On 17 February the National Assembly passed legislation to force us off the street. Along with other English institutions Dawson voted to defy the law for twenty-four hours. So it was back to Viger Street, this time to be photographed by police with telephoto lenses. Cars honked in support of us. A taxi driver yelled, "Good for you. Keep at it." Another man stopped and said, "This morning I'm embarrassed to speak French." Then the union pulled us in. Had all the colleges continued the strike, the government would probably have had to call an election. But the union heads backed Lévesque's separatist party and we were brutally punished for our resistance with a year's loss of seniority, which took a large slice from our future pensions, and a roll-back of the raise in salary we'd won under the terms of our previous contract. By then I'd had enough of Quebec politics.

✪✪✪

Beginning in 1988 I had five generous grants from the Social Sciences and Humanities Research Council of Canada to fund my scholarly work, each for three years. These highly competitive peer-reviewed grants were designed for university professors with paid sabbaticals, which the colleges did not provide, so while my expenses were amply covered, unlike a university teacher I was rarely able to get more than a few consecutive months away except on unpaid leave.

Nonetheless, Alan and I began to spend more time in London. We'd had a second year there when Nicholas was eight and went to Fitzjohn's School in Hampstead, the best he ever attended. Up at 7:30, we'd drop him at the school gate by 8:45, then walk for a good hour down to the British Museum, over Primrose Hill with its memories of the conspirator Titus Oates, and across a fine stretch of Regent's Park. After a morning's work there was lunch with our friends and more work. Then we'd take turns meeting Nicholas for tea at Louis's near the Hampstead Tube Station. Sundays the three of us would fly kites and play baseball on the Heath with Canadian friends Rufus and

Reet Gilday. It was pleasant to be always in that rhythm with very few distractions. By 1988 Nick was at university and whenever we could clear a term Alan and I went back to recharge our batteries.

At Dawson my responsibilities remained the same. For more than a decade I sat on the College Senate, where at the time all the broad educational decisions were made, and then on the Board of Governors for another six years. But I soon began teaching literature to the Liberal Arts students, who studied an integrated set of courses taught by colleagues whose familiarity with their disciplines was impressive, and who believed that it was everyone's responsibility to teach students to write well with careful research, empathy, and the beginnings of original perspective. The program was headed by historian Aaron Krishtalka who, as well as teaching history, was a brilliant administrator. As the bureaucratic noose tightened, he translated bureaucratese into English and vice versa, sparing us the plethora of performative paperwork that increasingly rained down. A group of Liberal Arts students who are now in their early forties told me recently the reason the program was so exciting was that in it they had peers who shared intellectual interests and teachers who had been, in their words, "knowledgeable characters" who worked them hard.

Graham Greene thought teaching to be the death of a writer, and as the political interference in our curriculum at Dawson grew I began to agree with him. But in academia there has always been an important synergy between teaching and research that fuels the imagination and freshens the classroom. I became vividly aware of this on 3 April 1991 when Judy Stoffman, then literary editor of the *Toronto Star*, rang me very early in the morning to say that Graham had died. I'd been reviewing books for her for a couple of years and she wanted me to write a half-page about him for the next day's broadsheet. She said she'd send a courier for it at five o'clock that afternoon and if I hadn't finished by then he'd wait. I was teaching *The Comedians* to my British Literature class that afternoon and thought to cancel it. Then, realizing the students would have heard the news, I decided to go.

I found them uncustomarily in the hall outside the classroom. Did I know that Graham Greene had died last night, Diane de Kerckhove asked. She soon won a Rhodes Scholarship, became a physicist and, when she returned from Oxford to Montreal for a year to devote herself to recording her music before taking up a teaching position at the University of Guelph, joined me on Dawson's Board of Governors. Diane knew that I had worked with Graham, but until then I hadn't told the other students. Instead of a lecture, I read them the draft of what I had written and asked if there was anything else I should say. For the next hour my research became the beating heart of the class. I'm sure most of the students had never connected scholarly work with what they were learning, and for many securing a decent grade on an essay was of more interest than what they were researching themselves. But that day their agenda changed, and so did mine. From then on I narrowed the professional distance between myself and students and told them about my writing, especially when it related to what they were studying.

❂❂❂

I never regretted teaching, but I did object to administrators who demanded more and more of our time and bureaucrats who meddled with the department's curriculum. Now, when despondent young colleagues ask me whether teaching literature even matters any more, I remind them of Fraser Kyle, for whom our department's prize was named. Fraser sat at my feet every class – literally – front row, centre aisle, Modern European Literature. That September I began with Tolstoy's *The Death of Ivan Ilyich* and, with Fraser's bald head in my field of vision, I measured the words of my first lecture with extreme care. I need not have, for as I guessed what his baldness meant, he knew my embarrassment. Before our second class I found him waiting outside my office. "I have cancer," he said, and as I nodded in recognition his face broke into a broad grin. "It's amazing what you get away with when your professors know."

What we read that term led us to talk often about the shortness of life and, although Fraser was my student, he was also my teacher. He knew haste. If he loaned me a book on an afternoon, I knew he'd be waiting for me at seven in the morning to discuss it. And as the months passed he spoke to his classmates about what we were studying with an immediacy, a wisdom, and a humour I could not match.

One day at the hospital a few weeks before he died he asked if I remembered how Ivan Ilyich's anger at the inevitability of his own death changed at the end of the story, how what he had first seen as blackness turned into light. I remembered well what Fraser had said at the time, that the change showed Ilyich's love for the people he was leaving behind. That day in hospital he asked if I would read something for him at his funeral, something I thought he'd like. And when I agreed he added, "I always understood Tolstoy's story. But now I know what Ilyich felt just before the end. We don't die. We live on in other people's lives."

There were several hundred in the church that day, including Fraser's classmates who, because of his openness during our literary discussions, had bonded tightly. I was asked to speak first and I read two pieces, beginning with a short passage from Tolstoy's *Childhood*. In it the young sensitive narrator looked at his dead mother's lifeless face as his imagination sketched for him "one picture after another of pulsing life and happiness." I knew its tenderness would make Fraser's mother cry. The roles reversed, how could she not? When I finished I waited until she looked up, then read for her a few of Fraser's favourite lines of poetry:

Some time, man or woman, traveller,
afterwards, when I am not alive,
look here, look for me here
between the stones and the ocean,
in the light storming
in the foam.
Look here, look for me here,
For here is where I shall come, saying nothing,
no voice, no mouth, pure,
here I shall be again the movement

of the water, of
its wild heart,
here I shall be both lost and found –
here I shall be perhaps both stone and silence.

When Nancy smiled at me through her grief I was sure Pablo Neruda had worked his magic, and I'd done what Fraser wanted. He had said he was an atheist, that there were to be no prayers at his funeral, no hymns, no religion. Yet, as if making a joke, he asked his parents to bury him with Dante's *The Divine Comedy* – "just in case."

Children always teach their parents, students their teachers, but they don't always teach us as much as Fraser – and his family – taught me that year about grace, generosity of spirit, and emotional honesty. Just before he died he was admitted into the honours English program at McGill, and the prize in his name has helped other young people do what he'd wanted to. Fraser knew that studying literature puts students into a larger narrative that encourages empathy and builds the capacity to explore and embrace independent and critical thinking – which is not to forget the life-long pleasure of a well-stocked imagination. I may have written less by teaching, and it certainly took me longer to begin writing steadily, but I learned in the classroom more than I would have written. And there is a sameness in bringing someone to life in biography and pulling a room of students together in literature.

In 2006, a few days after a man walked into the de Maisonneuve wing of Dawson on 13 September to murder eighteen-year-old Anastasia De Sousa and seriously injure nineteen other students, I stood at my classroom door and hugged each of my students when they returned to the college. It was near the beginning of term and we didn't know one another well but I hugged all thirty of them, nonetheless. I said nothing until the last one stood in front of me. He was well over six feet tall and as I looked up at him I smiled and said, "You don't want a hug too, do you?" He bent down and sobbed quietly in my ear, "Yes I do."

I suppose given today's political correctness I'd be fired for touching them and for joking, however mildly, about hugging the tall student who came last into the room. But they needed touch, and a little lightness, and the straight talk that followed about what had happened. When I asked at the beginning of the next class if they wanted to talk more about the shooting, they said no. They wanted to discuss what we were reading, which was Rebecca West's *The Return of the Soldier*. They seemed to understand that novel instinctively as they steeled their young selves to go on. Talking about the trauma in West's narrative put their own vulnerability into perspective.

I recently watched Amelia Sargisson, a student with whom I had read *Genesis* and discussed Milton, play Eve in the Stratford company's production of *Paradise Lost*. She spotted me in the audience and near the end of second bows waved to me in a very special literary acknowledgment. When I was in Toronto recently a lawyer neighbour of my son's told me he'd been a student at Dawson the year before I was hired and claimed that those were two of the best years of his life. He spoke loudly about what is still known as the Dawson approach to higher general education even if, now that the college is fifty years old, that generous habit of learning has been badly eroded.

Then there was the day I was standing on the corner of Mountain Street and de Maisonneuve with my neighbour Barbara Steinman, waiting for the light to change when a tall, half-bald man close to forty-five came up behind us and threw his arms around me. "It's Nick," he said. "Do you remember me?" I remembered him well, sitting in the back row with little interest in school and serious family problems. Like Ricky and Benny he had talked his way through many classes but unlike them, his attention was caught by literature. And there he was, an engineer who said, "You changed my life, you know. Thank you." Somehow he had learned to read like Charles Dickens's David Copperfield, who sat alone on his bed "reading as if for life."

4

Sigrun Bülow-Hübe
Just Tell the Truth

On an August afternoon in the mid-1980s when I was in Sutton and *The Dangerous Edge* and *Reflections* were on their way but not yet published, Tobie Steinhouse took me to Sigrun Bülow-Hübe's very Swedish house in nearby Brome for tea. One of Canada's finest print-makers, Tobie was in the Eastern Townships painting and wanted me to meet Sigrun who, Tobie said, had won many international prizes for her furniture designs. I knew Sigrun had furnished one of Moshe Safdie's Habitat apartments at Expo 67 and done the interior of Malmö's Stadsteater in Sweden, which had influenced Fred Lebensold's design for Place des Arts. As it turned out, our houses were only five miles apart.

Sigrun sat on a cloth-covered stool on one side of a teak coffee table, dropping her cigarette ash into a large copper pan. Her still blondish hair was tied back and she'd tucked a red scarf into the neck of her grey silk shirt. On her right wrist was an elegant silver bracelet that turned on itself in a Möbius loop to follow the outer side of her hand. She said her youngest sister, Torun, had designed it for Georg Jensen and that hers was the prototype.

I sat across from her on what I later learned was one of her prize-winning sofas, the light streaming down on us at a sharp angle from the clerestory windows behind her. She asked what I was writing and I told her about Charlotte Haldane for whose biography I had just found a publisher. I said I was having trouble with the book. Although *The Dangerous Edge* had been biographical in tracing Graham's political thinking, this was my first full-blown biography and I was still uneasy about the whole process of life-writing. Did I know Montrealer Irene Kon, a friend of hers who was also writing a biography? "Yes," I said. "I've just read the manuscript." "What do you think of it?" she wanted to know. I hesitated to answer. "And?" she insisted. "I thought it more like advertising copy than a book." "Thank God someone else had the courage to tell her," she cut in, and we were instant friends.

I soon began to take supper to Sigrun when I was alone in Sutton because she was old and unwell and I admired her straightforwardness. We would eat, then push the dishes aside and play gin rummy on the dining table. As the record player was on a shelf next to her chair, she usually chose what we listened to while we talked late into the night keeping a cumulative score, which eventually reached well into the thousands. Early on she played Purcell's *Dido and Aeneas*, directing throughout, "Now wait and you will hear … Now wait." Finally Kirsten Flagstad's rich voice came to "When I am laid in earth." I must have been visibly moved because, as Sigrun closed the record box, she pushed it across the table and said, "There. Now *you* have it." "But you will want it again," I said. "No, I will never listen to it again. It's yours." I pushed it back toward her and, as she replaced it on the shelf, she turned and said almost as a joke, "Play it when I die." When a couple of years later she took it down a second time, I asked if we would listen to it again. "No," she said, "You take it." And I did.

But even then I had no idea she would become so much a part of my life and writing that when she died in 1994 I began to live with the invisible. Like all people who mourn, I talked to her. I never actually saw her as some claim they do the dead, but I thought I smelled her cigarettes on occasion and, once caught by this possibility, opened her old books in search of another whiff and with it another story about her life.

"I never told anyone these stories," she said a couple of months after we met. "No one in Canada was ever interested." I was, although when she said it I didn't appreciate what her memories were germinating in me, any more than I knew when I met Graham Greene the benefit to me of not being allowed a tape recorder. Narratives are for finding out, and the more I listened to her woodwind voice the more eagerly I entered that autobiographical web of words she was confined to by age. Each of her stories opened a window and, as I saw things that were obvious but unrecognized, I slowly began to understand the complexities of writing biography.

✿✿✿

Sigrun had learned not to cry in 1919 a few weeks after she turned six. It was the winter of her first illness. Her mother had said only that she was being sent to her grandmother's island when she took her to the Stockholm train station and left her in the care of a strange woman. A newspaper had been bought for her to read on the train. In the seconds it took her mother to fade into the swirling snow Sigrun learned privacy. She covered her face with the paper and kept it there until the train stopped and she was led into the hotel in Tranås for the night.

With the light, a great wooden sled came to take her to Romanö, her family's rocky island in Lake Sommen. In the sled's seductive sway she forgot her illness. On the island there was a breakfast party with friends. The child laughed over her porridge and the attention of an older boy. Then suddenly she was betrayed again, this time by herself. In the acrid reek of vomit, safety vanished forever. That night she took refuge in her grandmother's arms in the ancestral bed where her body would mend. When her immediate family arrived for the summer her tubercular lesions had scarred over but even after the sun-filled days that followed she could not trust her body. The necessary delusion that she would be well forever was gone.

The night she told me this story it had rained for six days and she'd spent them in bed reading the six volumes I'd brought her of Virginia

Woolf's diaries. "I think of her death often," she said. "Of the stone. How big a stone do you need? Of her body exposed, floating in the reeds. Bloated. Purple. I won't go over it. I can't. I leave her coming quickly out of Monk's House, the letters left, her not then able to go back. I think of the cane by the river. No more. The rest is her privacy."

There was that word again. Privacy. "I leave her there," Sigrun said. But she couldn't. Neurosis, I thought, is the bodily manifestation of the despair of life. Just listen. As a fledgling biographer, I was good at listening, at paying attention to detail. And I had learned to wait. But I didn't yet know how to protect myself from other people's stories, something Sigrun had learned at six by covering her face with a newspaper. Although it seemed a contradiction in terms, I wondered if privacy – a proper distance – was an important lesson in biography. "She must have been determined to die," Sigrun said. "Suffocating under the water, held down by the stone. She must have been incredibly still. In a trance perhaps. It was also because of the war." With this change of direction Sigrun jumped up and tacked the bookmark photo of Virginia Woolf to the wall beside her bed.

She then told me about the recurrence of the TB when she was twenty-one and how she'd had to lie absolutely still for the next year in a sanatorium on the mainland within eyesight of Romanö. She had collapsed at a party given by a rich friend of her mother's who had told her since childhood that, if she behaved, she would be left various things she liked in the house. She had not wanted to attend the party but felt obliged by the woman's kindness. And she had been unable to eat her favourite supper there of salmon and potatoes boiled with fresh dill.

She had retreated upstairs to lie down on the floor, her belly filled again with tubercular fluid. The doctor had taken her to the hospital in an ambulance. In the theatre she could hear the clatter of surgical instruments and professional talk but her attention was focused on two small yolks of light. In her pain she struggled against choosing which of them to follow and concluded before her ethered sleep that it made no difference. There is no free will, she told the doctor when she woke. He said the fluid had hit the ceiling when he punctured her belly, then proudly declared that he had cleaned everything inside so she needn't worry about ever getting pregnant. Just like that.

"Have you read *The Magic Mountain*?" she asked. In the sanatorium you could not move, even to hold a book. They came once a week and opened the incision again to drain it. Now we will see what kind of a person you are, the doctor would warn as he cut. She held the bed rails above her head and closed her eyes to protect herself. "Young people died there," she said. "You never asked what had happened when someone vanished. You just knew. When you were well enough, they put you outside for the day even in winter. The birds came to eat off your tray."

From the age of three she had known about the shed where the patients lay. She and her sister Gunlög, who was two years older, had passed it every day in the summer when they went to get the milk and mail. They rowed from Romanö to the mainland and walked through the farm attached to the sanatorium. The path through the woods was dark. Then came the shed at the back of the building. On a rainy day the mattresses were folded over to keep dry under the roof. Otherwise the patients lay there, bundled. In the woods Sigrun sometimes met people walking slowly, silently, dark undefined figures that foreshadowed her future. But she was just a child on a daily mission with her sister, innocently carrying the bacillus that infected her intestine back to their island paradise.

While she was an inmate her reserved father, Erik, came to the sanatorium to give her his greatest treasure; she kept his Viking bowl on the shelf above the record player in Brome. When he took her back to her Stockholm apartment, she wasn't quite well. He stayed with her for the night, and in the morning she found caviar, tinned asparagus, and other French delicacies on her counter from the most expensive shop in Gamla Stan. She had studied with Kaare Klint in Copenhagen at the School of Architecture in Det Kongelige Danske Kunstakademi, and when Erik returned he brought her a pamphlet he'd written inscribed, "To my colleague from the author."

His father had gone to America to seek his fortune when Erik was a boy and never returned. When the letters stopped coming, his mother assumed he'd been murdered or met some other tragic death and married her lonely cousin, joining their names to become Bülow-Hübe. "Do not rely on a husband," Erik told his three daughters from a young age. "You must have a profession."

Sigrun's mother, Runa, had grown up on Romanö. She was the seventh and youngest child of Sweden's famous painter Knut Ekwall and his German wife, Theresia Burkowitz-Pönitz, who sang chamber music. When the children were old enough she formed them into a chamber group to accompany her on short winter tours. Sigrun showed me a book that Runa had written in 1907 for her own mother when she and Erik became engaged two weeks after they met. He was eleven years her elder, a very shy architect. Runa was sixteen, the blond darling of the family, and her mother was worried. So Runa wrote the book in verse as a kind of appeasement to Theresia and illustrated it with caricatured likenesses to explain how she and Erik had met and fallen in love.

It seemed that Runa had grown up in an almost mythical environment of creativity and self-sufficiency. As Sigrun talked about her own summers on the island I came to know it as an unchanging magical place. The photo album she pulled out in which some of the pictures had been taken with Ekwall's homemade camera held scenes of the three generations sailing, sunning on the rocks, swimming, gathering flowers in the woods, and picking wild berries to press and ferment for fruit wine. Even in recent pictures her grandfather's romantic paintings still hung in the house and her mother's sculptures stood boldly against the idyllic landscape. The photos looked like set shots for *Wild Strawberries*.

Life in Malmö, where the family moved from Saltsjöbaden when Erik became director of town planning there, was different. "Ours were ideal parents," Sigrun insisted. "They were never around!" Erik was always working, and Runa had been so protected from danger that she never passed on negative warnings about the world to her children. She was a child herself when Gunlög and Sigrun were born and too young to have a vision for them that they would have to escape. They saw her one afternoon on her way to meet friends with their record player under one arm and its trumpet on her head like a hat. She was beautiful and charming and, Sigrun said, very spoiled.

Sigrun's brother, Staffan, was younger than she and Gunlög. He had accidents. One day when the only adult around was the cook he shot himself playing with Erik's First World War air pistol. Gunlög washed the blood off his mouth, pressed the bullet out of his cheek and bandaged him up. Another day he boiled dirt and stones and water on the stove to feed a rat he'd seen in the garden, then stepped into the cooling pot by accident and skinned his leg.

"Of course Gunlög and I had accidents too," Sigrun said, "but they were different. We saw things we probably shouldn't have, boys writing words we didn't understand on walls and drawing pictures of genitals, always women's. We thought them hurtful but weren't quite sure how and never told our parents. We saw men masturbating in the park. Gunlög decided they had to milk themselves like cows," she laughed. "We read whatever we wanted in Erik's study and went to concerts with Runa." Sigrun had a natural and well-schooled musical ear. She could unfailingly tell what key a piece was in and quickly identify its composer. She had sung hymns at school and still remembered swaths of the New Testament she'd been made to memorize. But there was no mention of God at home. Still, as she got sicker I could hear twinges of Sweden's Lutheran guilt in her factual honesty.

❁❁❁

Sigrun told me about Berlin in late 1933 when Hitler's brownshirts were spreading violent anti-semitism on the streets and already rounding people up. A distant cousin who lived there and had taken her to cabarets was later murdered in the Holocaust. Brecht and Weill had left Germany earlier that year but in some places Weill's music was still played. She saw a disguised *Die Dreigroschenoper*. The Threepenny set rotated, she said, and could be switched almost instantly if Nazis entered.

And she told me about her small Stockholm apartment in Gamla Stan where during the war internationally known architects, painters, writers, and intellectuals who had sought refuge in Sweden gathered. It was in a fifteenth-century building just off Västerlånggatan. One window looked across the street to the square; the other opened onto Kökbrinken. When you came in from that narrow street you walked up slender stone steps that curved to the flat and dipped in the middle from centuries of wear. Each had a different flower carved in it.

From there she and her friend, the painter Adja Yunkers, had run the handmade magazines *ARS* and *CREATION*. Just after the war they invited T.S. Eliot to Stockholm to read *The Wasteland*. They had no idea how large an audience he'd draw, and so many people came that even the square outside the restaurant they'd rented was packed. Eliot read as Sigrun had never heard anyone read before, with exactness to cadence and the poem's changing voices. He made them live, she said. A few years after she told me this, I heard Eileen Atkins recite *The Wasteland* at the Rialto Theatre in Montreal. I was so impressed with the similarity of her reading to what Sigrun had told me of Eliot's that I went backstage after the performance to tell her. Although Sigrun didn't understand all of the poem, she said it was like a breathing animal. "Remember Phlebas?" she asked, and without waiting for my answer got up to find a newspaper picture of herself sitting next to Eliot at dinner. She was beautiful but claimed she had never wished to be. She had wanted to be sophisticated, elegant, intelligent, and private and in her hat and dark-rimmed glasses she looked all of that. She said she had never felt so much a schoolgirl, knowing little about British poetry then and being still very shy. "If I'd only known what I know now I could have asked him about Virginia Woolf, but I didn't and we were both uncomfortable."

She had been competing with men all her life. She'd had many lovers and she'd also had to hold her own in an intensely male world. She laughed as she told me that one day shortly after the war when she was at lunch in Stockholm's Restaurang Cattelin several well-known European members of her profession joined the architect's table to talk about public housing. As usual she was the only woman there and she ate silently as she listened to high praise of her work. Then one of the great men asked if she knew where he might find the fellow responsible for it. "Yes," she replied. "I am he!"

Soon afterward she got into a prolonged debate about the public responsibility of architects. By then she had gained wide recognition as chief interior designer of Malmö's Stadsteater, the building that influenced Fred Lebensold's design of the Queen Elizabeth Theatre in Vancouver as well as Montreal's Place des Arts, won first prize in Sweden's National Wallpaper Competition, a gold medal at the Exposition Internationale de l'Urbanisme in Paris, and driven alone across postwar America on a scholarship to study the production methods of prefabricated houses and mass-produced furniture. She thought her colleagues' social spirit dwindling. When they mocked her and suggested she take a job advertised by the European office of the T. Eaton Company for a design consultant in Montreal she impulsively took it. Not that attitudes were different here, but she found such a scarcity of well-designed furniture in the city that she couldn't resist the challenge to stay. In 1953 she had gone into partnership with a small factory started by Estonian immigrants to form AKA, where she remained chief designer until after Expo 67. By then she had won twelve of Canada's National Industrial Design Council awards for her furniture and taken part in several other international exhibits and world fairs. The thousands of her design and architectural plans now form her Archive in McGill University's John Bland Canadian Architecture Collection of papers.

❂❂❂

As she got sicker Sigrun would sit in bed all day reading the library books I brought her, seven a week. She wanted only biographies now, to know how other people had lived and what they had learned. If I was there on a Sunday morning we'd talk about the books until late afternoon. Time became irrelevant because it had nowhere to go. Only our conversation had meaning. Only the stories, although I still had no idea where they were leading me, which means that I could still see no clear direction with Charlotte Haldane.

Her fiction was autobiographical and I knew that the problem with it was the lack of space between her novelist and autobiographical selves. My problem with her was how to separate the two. I needed the details from the stories she had woven around herself but I needed to select them for reliability. And as I did I knew I was refocusing and clipping them toward my own image of her, just as I was forming my own image of Sigrun from the stories she was telling me. Should I then conceal myself in recreating Charlotte's life or be honest about my position as I pulled its fragments together?

"If my father had not had all those old books in his study, and if you had not spent your young Saturdays going around Montreal with Fred Lebensold looking at his buildings, this would never have happened," Sigrun said. Despite the difference in our ages, the coincidences of our lives were certainly many. We had met by accident that summer afternoon but our paths had crossed for decades. In the early fifties when she lived in a flat on Barclay Avenue I had just moved to de Roquancourt a quarter of a mile away. One evening at the Lebensolds' house in the early sixties I had overheard Fred talking to her at the front door. She was then working with him at Place des Arts and at McGill. He didn't invite her in as he usually did his colleagues. He said she was the very best at everything she did but she was a tough cookie. "They always called me a tough cookie behind my back," Sigrun laughed.

When her much younger silversmith sister, Torun, found out about these overlaps she shouted, "You see. I knew there was something to it." Synchronicity, she called our friendship. I thought it luck, with the additional benefit for me of raising important questions about life-writing. Sigrun said its honesty was rare. This coincidental stuff, Swedish or otherwise, became more intense after the melanoma Sigrun had lived with from before I knew her turned up in her pancreas and liver. When she found out she was furious. "I told you I wouldn't die from lung cancer," she admonished her doctors in controlled anger as she stopped beside the oxygen tanks in the emergency department at the Cowansville hospital and lit a cigarette. I stayed with her that weekend. We spent most of it in the past going over the same stories. When she'd apologize for the repetition, another memory would surface almost as recompense.

Copenhagen, 1939. New Year's Eve. In the largest department store in the city there was a room on the sixth floor with small tables elegantly set with white cloths for tea, and a dance floor with a very good orchestra. Her tea, toast, and marmalade arrived. So did a man who continued to circle her table. The rules of a *thé dansant* were very strict. The man must not ask you to dance while you ate and you must dance with him when he did. Sigrun drank her tea slowly, then lit a cigarette as he came to claim her. They discovered a mutual acquaintance in Stockholm, someone she did not like. When the music stopped as the afternoon lengthened, he suggested they continue at a place he knew around the corner.

It was in a small room. There were five stools at a bar in the front and a restaurant at the back where a Danish family were having a party in silly paper hats. They had a drink. Then she remembered, "I have an appointment. What time is it?" "Haven't you got a watch?" he asked. He rummaged in his pocket, pulled one out, and put it on her wrist. She laughed and said, "I can't take a gift like that from a stranger." He showed her his own watch, exactly the same. "I have a watch business."

They walked across Knippels Bridge onto the quay. It was snowing. Because the streets were deserted you could see the backbone of the city. Against it she felt as grotesque as the family in the bar had looked in their party hats. It was wartime. As they walked along he suddenly turned to her and said, "Thank you for this afternoon. It has been very enjoyable for me," turned again and walked away. "I stood there watching him go," she said, "watching his footprints in the snow, black as they melted in the mild air and remained melted holes. He never looked back. I waited until his figure vanished." Almost without a pause she laughed at the theatrically of his exit. It was the perfect ending for a war film. "Time had run out," she said as she took the watch off her wrist and put it on mine.

From that day Sigrun's watch ran slow. We all connect things, marking coincidences as naturally as Shakespeare married an aging body to the bare ruined choirs of late autumn trees. I was no poet, but Sigrun's running-down watch kept me longer in Sutton than I might otherwise have stayed and in the time left I came to fully appreciate the precious knot between a biographer and her subject, and to finally understand its necessary looseness – the silence of privacy. "Just tell the truth," Sigrun would say when I'd close the door on her stories to take up Charlotte Haldane's life. "It's the detail you want. If you try to understand things they will slip away from you."

⭘⭘⭘

Every so often her despair broke through. "I'm finished," she would shout. "It's happened so suddenly. Only a month ago I had energy. Now the pain is constant." But in telling me about her life she always rallied. There was an urgency now. "Have I given you some stories?" she wanted to know. "If we had never met you would have finished your book, maybe written another." That was a big maybe. "I'll finish Charlotte's biography when you die," I replied. "This is more important." I was going through menopause by then and losing something of myself in that transition. "You have given me my middle years," I told her. She smiled and nodded. "I left Sweden behind when I came here. I never talked about it. It died for me because no one understood. You have brought it to life." "I just listened," I said. "Your stories live in me now." Was there comfort in that, I wondered. I also wondered, although I never said it, how to release myself from her stories. "I hope the melanoma doesn't live in you too," she said. I knew that for someone who had spent her life solving spatial problems precisely, feeling diseased must have been particularly hard. She hated messiness.

Added to the reason she came to Montreal was the end of a long love affair with the only man she might have married had he not already got a wife. He too was an architect and her intellectual equal. Her photos showed him to be a beautiful man and his house beside the sea a modern embodiment of Romanö. When people asked why she stayed in Montreal in the early fifties when artists were given little recognition and no one knew what an industrial designer was, she would say there were enormous opportunities here. But as she quickly learned, Montrealers didn't like foreigners showing them new ways to do things, especially brainy women. Sigrun had stayed because to leave would have been a messy defeat and she had strong professional pride.

There had been dreadful setbacks. A fire in the factory one winter was the worst. The machinery was saved only because it froze in the water and was later thawed by her partners in a controlled way without rust damage. Luckily for her, a second generation of immigrants were moving up in the city and had enough money to buy furniture from AKA. By 1967 when the ergonomic simplicity of her designs had become so fashionable that she was asked to furnish one of Moshe Safdie's Habitat apartments at Expo, she was exhausted and turned twenty years of honest work into a civil servant's job setting up Design Canada in Ottawa with a small indexed pension. From there, and with considerable humour since she rarely cooked herself, she showed male manufacturers how to design kitchens ergonomically suited to their wives, and set up a scholarship program to send young women to the world's top design schools.

After the weekend when she gave me her watch there was a necessity on both our parts to maintain the future in present habits. Sigrun recorded even more fastidiously than before the temperature and other daily details on her calendar. She also kept a list of everything she read in a green book. On Thursday, 28 April 1994, two bluebirds tested the new birdhouse Alan had put outside the kitchen window for her. The female went in and out several times while the male sat on the tree behind. "Write it down," she said. "We must write it down." She took her black pen, then a blue one, then changed her mind again. "No. We need red." And so the bluebirds were recorded on the calendar in capital red letters.

For my part I needed her to eat. When she stayed in bed I lured her to the kitchen by reporting that the daffodils were coming up on the bank behind the bird house. I had tried for several years to get bulbs to grow there but either the squirrels ate them or they'd been consumed by the eroding earth and dropped down between the tree roots that held the steep bank in place. As they rose that last spring from the dark wet soil, she inscribed their translucence in her record while I recorded her final stories in my notebook alongside biographical notes about Charlotte.

❂❂❂

Hers would be a very Swedish death. Through his camera Bergman would have smiled on the scenes, which needed no editing, no revision of dialogue for effect. The cast could be caught in one frame. There was Sigrun's loved but sometimes irritating younger sister, Torun, and myself. "No more sisters, no more sisters," Sigrun had shouted when she dropped the receiver for the last time on her older sister, Gunlög, the day before Torun arrived from Copenhagen to hasten Sigrun away from her last remaining escape – telling me the stories that had become our privacy.

Is honesty always the best way? It was difficult at that point for me to know. Torun was a brilliant and powerful silversmith, the pride of Georg Jensen, and of Sigrun. And after Sigrun died we became close friends. She charmed everyone, was invariably generous and fun, always appreciative and kind. But Sigrun's rationality and intelligence so terrified her that as soon as she arrived she recited prayers to protect herself until I stopped her. As a schoolgirl during the war she'd had the courage to sail her boat across the sound from Malmö in the dark to rescue Jews from Denmark. But when Sigrun died she was so afraid of being in the house alone that she spent the better part of the next two months in ours. Had I told her that her sister didn't want her to come, Sigrun might have lived a few days longer. But I was too frightened of what damage it would do if I said so.

The night before she arrived, Sigrun had wakened me with a dream. Perhaps night is not the best word, but what other is there for that dark passage through quicksand that sucks the dying and their attendants into the final hourglass? She had found herself among hundreds of little people, dressed like them in an ankle-length woolly sweater with a cowl that was pulled up over her head. They were making a clicking noise with their teeth. It drove her crazy. It was pre-language, she said, and she could not stop herself making the same noise as she decided what to take with her on the journey. Everything was sparse. Everyone had just enough paper to wrap a small bundle, "this way and that way," she indicated with her accurate architect's hands showing the over-lapping papers, "and just enough string." You had to take with you something that would identify you when you got where you were going, not to someone else but to yourself. She didn't know what she was placing in her small bundle, and she didn't want to join the moving line. But she knew she had to follow its incessant shuffle.

The inventiveness of her dream was no surprise to me, nor it's meaning. People do see their own deaths near the end and she'd had another dream shortly before. In it she had given everything away including the house, and had dug and climbed into her grave. "But I couldn't figure out how to cover myself up," she had told me in laughter. That too was a death dream but it was also a design problem she was trying to solve. This dream was different. That it was imagined as a wandering toward somewhere, even coming as it did from an immigrant approaching her final embarkation, startled me. I had believed that in sharing with me all the necessary departures that made up her story Sigrun had by some Freudian process arrived at a kind of acceptance of her own demise. That there was another obvious interpretation confused me because I knew her to be an atheist. And it bothered me that several times on her last day she took hold of my hand and said "Förlåt mig." My assurance that she had done nothing that needed to be forgiven had no power against the hideous shuffle in her dream.

Or was there nothing Christian in it? Did she want forgiveness for having entrapped me in her stories, stories that were now mine? "Don't let the family catch you too," she had also said near the end. "You must get away from them." Alan had often wished he could speak with her crystalline clarity and I knew her to be incapable of obfuscation. There was no place in her for emotional sloppiness. Her intellectual precision was a combination of the highest aesthetic and ethical standards tempered by a broad sympathy for human frailty and a deep humility. But we are the product of the stories we tell ourselves, not their source. Romanö was her prison as well as her idyll.

"Just tell the truth," Sigrun had said. But what is the truth of someone's life? And from the mass of detail you need and want to keep, how should it be remembered? With precision and sympathetic care, of course, an intimacy even. And also, as I had come to appreciate, with a proper distance. But entering into another life is a complex thing and the gap of privacy between a life and biographical truth is deeper than I was ready for that day.

When I went back to the house I sat alone and scanned her living room in an attempt to save its warmth and colour in memory. The ceiling was of four-inch boards, yellowed with age and cigarette smoke. Pine, spruce? Tongue and groove, each abutment in the middle of the next row running from east to west up to the peak of fifteen feet, maybe sixteen. Below it were thick crossing rafters, secured together with bolts. The windows went to the roof of the dining wall on the east side. Below them on the shelf were a couple of large papier mâché bowls we had made together from the *Globe and Mail*. Thirty-one, all differently painted, had stood against the window one Christmas ready to be given as presents. On the west wall in the corner where it met the north wall and the windows sat her drawing table, its set rule in place from her last project. She had hurried from her sick bed one night to design an extension she'd promised Alan for our Sutton house. She'd puzzled over it in her mind for weeks, then wondered why it had taken her so long.

The white walls dropped lightly beneath that wooden warmth and the celestial window-light. Everywhere, even on the doors, hangings told her story. From the central rafter hung the large loom she'd made years ago on which there was work that would never be finished. There were Adja Yunkers prints and paintings and her own woven pieces, bright in colour and design. Deep red irregular circles dropped one from the other, ceiling to floor on one canvas backing. On another, yellow and black wool swirled into a red vortex. The south wall had three panes of sliding glass that opened onto the deck, which was hinged to the house with twisted iron brackets she'd had the Sutton blacksmith make. We had often breakfasted on the deck and more often looked past it into the woods as we talked and played gin rummy on a summer's night. I locked the door and went home to listen to Kirsten Flagstad.

In a breath the silence begins, the last I love yous lost to its power. I looked in her eyes to find again the blueness of life, then closed them quickly not to expose her. The shroud was whiter than the ashes that spilled from my fingers onto the hill above her house. They burned the grass. But when you think someone's dead that's not always the case. "Some people have stories and can't write them," Sigrun said. "And some people have none and can write. Have you enough stories now?"

5

Charlotte Haldane

With and Without Husband JBS

The journalist and novelist Charlotte Franken Haldane was born in 1894. I became interested in her and several other little-known women writers of her generation when I was finishing *The Dangerous Edge* and decided to include her in a prosopography. As well as Charlotte, that book would have included Amabel Williams-Ellis, who was born the same year, Margaret Haig Thomas (Lady Rhondda), born the year before, and Margot Heinemann and Sheila Grant Duff, who were both born in 1913, the same year as Sigrun Bülow-Hübe. Throughout my Graham Greene research the names of such women kept turning up, usually as someone's wife who wrote or painted or was politically active. Charlotte had been written down as abrasive, tough-minded, and sexually free. These were not compliments in her generation, and still aren't.

George and Doreen Rudé had met Charlotte, and George had known her husband, the geneticist J.B.S. Haldane. In the early 1990s Doreen said she would gather some people for me to talk to about the Haldanes on my next research trip. By then the Rudés had left Monreal and were living at 24 Cadborough Cliff in Rye, which became my home away from home when I was on my own in England. From the back of the house you could watch the merchant vessels and sailboats move slowly across the shimmering horizon of the English Channel. The distant view was interrupted only by sheep huddled on the broad pastures of the Brede level far below the house and by Camber Castle, built for Henry VIII to protect Rye Harbour from the French and now beached among grazing sheep like a child's sand fort. At night a simple strand of lights on the road between Rye and the town of Winchelsea lit the empty space.

White roses climbed to the roof outside my bedroom window. They attracted bees and warblers. But it was the gulls rising early over the lip of the cliff at the bottom of the garden that woke me, and the magpies. Without washing I would walk down the Udimore Road toward Rye's red roofs stacked one above the other to the top of the hill perched over Romney Marsh. Before the hubbub began, the cobbled streets between the half-timbered cottages and Queen Anne houses were deserted. Even the harbour was quiet, the fishing boats still caught by low tide in the mud. Back up the hill George would be waiting for me to make coffee and to sit with him in the dining room window seat to talk about his work.

In the afternoon Doreen and I would drive through the leafy lanes toward Winchelsea or head for Camber Sands to put our feet in the salt water. Sometimes we'd drive to Dungeness to eat fish and chips at the Pilot and on the way back walk along the shingle beach to see what the fishermen had caught with their long flexible sea rods, and to find spitting stones. If you held one at arm's length and succeeded in spitting through the hole, legend was that your wish would be granted.

In the evenings there were dinner parties. Locals arrived on foot, Londoners came down in the afternoon and stayed the night. One was Cyril Andrews. Before the war he and Doreen had shared a cave in the rocks near Saint-Tropez with a few other young people and sponged off the wealthy. "After you got invited onto one boat you were passed from party to party and lived for nothing," Cyril said. There they met Patsy Willson. When the Second World War broke out she and Doreen were in Capri staying with Laetitia Cerio, whose father had owned the Villa Rosaio before Alexander Korda bought it for Graham Greene in part payment for the script of *The Third Man*.

Doreen said that Cyril had won two Military Crosses in the war and at its end had gone off with his colonel to Egypt. By the sixties he'd divorced his wife and was living in St John's Wood with Walter Gerstle, who had designed costumes for Marlene Dietrich and dresses for Carin, Hermann Göring's Swedish first wife. Cyril said she had saved many from arrest before she died in 1931, in the same manner that she saved Gerstle when he was living in Berlin. She told him there was going to be a putsch and that his name was on the list. He was to leave his flat next morning with only his satchel as though he were going to work and go instead to Budapest. There he was met by a man who gave him a train ticket to London and the number of a bank account that had been opened in his name. From it he received £5 a month for the rest of his life. But one never knew if Cyril's stories were quite true.

Another evening a distant neighbour turned up with her brother-in-law from Berkhamsted. He said that when *The Human Factor* was being filmed the crew had stayed in the town and their bill had not been paid. But the film had put Berkhamsted on the map and the town now realized it could cash in on being Graham's birthplace. That was 1982. Many years later when I was sick in Montreal with flu I was called by David Pearce, who was in charge of the Graham Greene Festival. Would I come to Berkhamsted and talk about Graham's women? "No," I said. After several more nos I added that I was sick and had to hang up. "Well just say yes and you can get back to bed," David laughed. "OK," I said, "but only about Graham's fictional women."

The next year I watched Graham's daughter, Caroline, as I finished the talk. Aunt Augusta is the only woman Graham ever let come close to narrating one of his novels and she was central in my discussion. After reviewing his other female characters unfavourably I discussed *Travels with My Aunt* at length and ended with a joke – with Aunt Augusta hurrying down the platform at Euston Station to catch the Berkhamsted train. Behind her I had a tall slightly stooped porter carrying her red suitcase. They looked into one another's eyes, hers sea-deep blue, his a lighter watery blue with a magnetic transparency you never forget. As Caroline realized that he was Graham, her serious face broke into an uncertain smile, then an astonished one, and then she roared with laughter as did everyone in the auditorium. I had to pull the mic to my mouth so my invented farewell from Aunt Augusta to the porter could be heard, and on the rising hilarity I became almost as permanent a fixture at the festival as Caroline. "The Long Wait for Aunt Augusta" was soon published by the Greene Trust and it has been republished in many other places since.

Dinner conversation at the Rudés' was either irreverently political or almost fantastical. If it veered to Ireland, Doreen would tell about singing as a girl with James Joyce, or if to Paris about being there with Elsie Innis, a friend with whom she and George had shared a house in Strand-on-the-Green during the war. Historian Richard Cobb had been invited to lunch and Elsie had gone out to get a baguette. Cobb arrived with another man, the son of a famous Irish rheumatologist. Doreen had heard that thirty years earlier this man had murdered his mother. As rumour had it, he'd chopped her in pieces and thrown her into the Bay of Killarney. Her body was never found and, since he was only seventeen and his father was who he was, he'd been sent to a reform school rather than prison. Doreen told him that her mother had known his father in Dublin. She said nothing about his mother but the man added that every terrible thing people said about him was true. Suddenly Elsie burst into the flat. The boy upstairs had killed his mother and father, and the police were on their way. "*Both* of them!" the fellow whooped in admiration.

✪✪✪

As promised when I began the research for Charlotte Haldane's biography, Doreen gathered some old communist friends for me to meet. George sometimes regaled a dinner with stories about the British party that were funny in the retelling, but he was rather oblique if I asked for organizational detail. Everyone knew that, decades earlier when he'd been giving a public talk on behalf of the party in London, one of his St Paul's School students had come by with his father – Lord somebody – and said, "Hello Sir," to George, who was shortly dismissed from his teaching job. He ended up in a comprehensive school until historian Hugh Stretton gave him a university position in Adelaide, Australia, where he taught for many years before coming to Sir George Williams. So I was pleased when Doreen, who, unlike George, had never been a communist and didn't even vote Labour at that time, invited these friends to a Rye lunch. Together they told me about the party's structure, about J.B.S. Haldane, Charlotte, and other prominent communist women they'd known.

Born in Sydenham to Jewish immigrants, Charlotte Franken was older than the Rudés' friends. But between them they knew she had started school in South Hampstead and then in 1906 moved with her family to Antwerp where, she said, she first experienced anti-semitism. When the family returned to London four years later, Charlotte had wanted to study languages at Bedford College for Women but her father's fur business failed and she was sent instead to secretarial school.

She worked for a concert agency by day and translated Anna Pavlova's ballet synopses at night. With war her father was declared an enemy alien. He escaped internment by fleeing to America with her mother, who had relatives there. Charlotte moved in with Ellen Tuckfield, who played the piano for Pavlova's rehearsals, disguised her German name as Franklyn, and began to publish stories. She was taken on as social editor of the *Daily Express*, then put in charge of the leader page and the correspondence column. By 1920 she'd become a full-fledged reporter and was writing weekend columns for the *Sunday Express*. Enter J.B.S. Haldane, with whom she fell in love when she went to Cambridge to interview him in 1924. She was then Charlotte Burghes, having married Ellen's attractive and penniless cousin Jack Burghes in 1918 when she was three months pregnant. She and JBS married in 1926.

The Rudés' friends had known her son, Ronald, but didn't know where he was. They said he'd joined the party before Charlotte so that he could go to Spain to fight Franco's fascists. She had gone later, as Paul Robson's guide and interpreter. When Germany attacked the Soviet Union she'd signed on with the *Daily Sketch* to travel with the first convoy of journalists to Russia. Like so many others, Charlotte had become a party member to fight fascism, and her sympathies were severely challenged by what she saw in Stalin's Russia. The day she returned to London she'd had a voluble fight with Party Secretary Harry Pollitt and resigned.

On the morning after our lunch, George talked. He explained how the party cells worked and that JBS had been prevented from divorcing Charlotte when she'd wanted to get out of the marriage in 1938. Pollitt had claimed the party couldn't stand the adverse publicity of two public people divorcing. George said that before then JBS had been a crypto-communist but when Charlotte defected he was told to broadcast his party affiliation and later to divorce her. Pollitt had then used the fact that she'd returned from Russia without the interview the *Daily Sketch* had hoped she'd get with Stalin to cast her in a sexist way. Rumour spread that the interview had been denied because Stalin "preferred to run the Soviet Union than to run Charlotte."

In her account of the trip, published as *Russian Newsreel* in 1942, Charlotte held her tongue about leaving the party and praised the Russian people's heroic effort against the Nazis. Her disillusionment with Stalin's communism and her anger about the lies she'd been told by Pollitt and the British party would wait until *Truth Will Out* in 1949. But in 1942 the party hadn't trusted her to keep quiet, George said, and, probably in retaliation for her defection, had her ties with Fleet Street cut. She was left almost penniless.

❂❂❂

So my hunt for Charlotte Haldane began. I had earned my spurs writing about Graham but that work hadn't involved the same kind of extensive primary biographical research away from the British Library that this did, and for several years of it I was teaching full time and relying on quick London trips. The book was long in coming even though I was lucky from the beginning.

Once the Rudés' friends told me the name of Charlotte's son it took only an archival hour to find his birth date and, more important, that there was no death record. But I had to leave London without finding out where he lived. After checking in at Heathrow I rang Doreen as I always did to say goodbye. Hanging in the telephone kiosk was a London directory containing only a handful of Burgheses; the name had seemed to me so common that I hadn't thought to look Ronald up in such a logical place. I rang the listing and Charlotte's granddaughter Louie answered. Ronnie was out of town and would phone me in Montreal when he got back.

On my next trip I went to the Marx Library in Clerkenwell. Folders had been put out for me about Charlotte's journey to China to represent the Women's World Committee for Peace and Democracy, and about the International Brigade's Dependents and Wounded Aid Committee of which she was the honorary secretary. I perused several other British Battalion files and had tea with a few women who'd known Charlotte and had kindly come to the library to talk with me. They said she'd been bossy and they clearly disliked her. She'd moved in intellectual circles, which they didn't trust, although they revered JBS. Charlotte had affairs, which further irritated them. "Charlotte the harlot," they'd called her in private. And she was a foreigner, by which they meant she was Jewish. This was my first whiff of antisemitism in London and I didn't let it go. They did admit what Doreen had said about the party's then serious misogyny. That established, they gave Charlotte grudging credit for her hard work, for what she had done for the Basque refugee children, and for standing up for women's rights in her journalism. Another cup of tea and they even praised her for arguing on principle against the party's then domination by its male leaders. They gave me their telephone numbers and got a good-looking fellow who worked in the library to drive me on his motorcycle through the traffic back to my Bloomsbury hotel.

He told me to get in touch with George Matthews at the party archive, which was in a warehouse in east London in a kind of industrial wasteland. When I arrived at the isolated train station, there were two men in sight, shooting up drugs at the end of the platform. I went quickly past them onto the road that ran through the adjoining fields and several empty streets, and then headed toward a derelict brick building about a quarter of a mile away. It was the only time I was ever frightened in London, where I'd walked alone at night for years from theatres and restaurants and friends' flats. Even after a spate of IRA bombings when Londoners were fearful, I had continued to go about alone until late one night as I was leaving Charing Cross Station, a taxi driver insisted on taking me to my hotel in Bloomsbury. He said he'd seen two muggings that day, and an earlier passenger had seen a man pull out a knife in Trafalgar Square and cut the head off a pigeon. He kept an illegal hammer under a towel on the seat beside him, and he told me never to walk alone at night. Evidently there was so much crime in London in those days that taxis had decided to take women passengers even if they couldn't pay.

The junkies followed at a distance, then began to catch up, and I ran the long last half block hoping that the bell would be answered quickly. No one came. I rang several times before I heard someone descend the steep inside stairs and the door was opened by Matthews, who stood on two canes. When we got upstairs, he apologized for the cold and said he hadn't been able to find much about Charlotte. He sat me in front of a couple of thin folders in which there was nothing of any importance. I said I had hoped to find more. Did he know George Rudé? Suddenly many boxes of papers appeared, along with a mug of tea and a heater that was so hot it almost burned my stockings.

Matthews was a charming and helpful fellow, and only after that day did I begin to appreciate the necessary secretiveness of party membership. I knew that George's intellectual ties with the party continued, although he said he hadn't paid his dues for some years. Alan had told me he thought that true of Eric Hobsbawm as well, although Eric's connection had remained closer. When George died in 1993 we met what appeared to be the last members of the old party at his funeral in Hastings. Because George had been on neighbourly terms with Rye's Church of England rector, Doreen had asked the man to conduct the funeral and to read a large part of Milton's "Lycidas" – which he did badly. He had promised her no religion but he peppered the proceedings with Christianity. Finally Eric spoke and with forceful enunciation: "George Rudé was a com-mun-ist. George Rudé was an a-the-ist." He gave an account of George's life, the high price he'd paid for his party connection, and the enormous respect historians of all political stripes had for his many books. The day I met Matthews I hadn't understood how deeply Charlotte had suffered from what Pollitt did when she left the party. In Hastings I saw its antithesis when, for no other reason than revenge, the rector tried to expunge Eric's eulogy with religious flummery as he committed George to the flames.

Unfortunately for my search, Charlotte had asked John Morris, her friend of many decades, to destroy her papers. He had been a member of the 1922 Mount Everest expedition and in 1936 on the Rutledge expedition had conducted telepathic experiments with her and her son.

Things always go missing from the biographical record but this was a huge loss. JBS's sister, the novelist Naomi Mitchison, had deposited his papers in the Bloomsbury Science Library at University College in London. They'd been heavily vetted but the divorce and some financial papers were there and Naomi was helpful in telling me about her relations with her brother and saying she thought Ronnie had had a rough time with him as a stepfather. I was astonished by her openness about her incestuous feelings for JBS although not by her suspicion that he was impotent, which I eventually confirmed, and which in part explained Charlotte's several affairs and certainly why the otherwise non-conformist JBS wouldn't sleep with her before they married.

In the BBC's written archive at Caversham, which the new generation of scholars is only now beginning to trawl, I found letters from Charlotte's immediate post-defection years when she'd made a living working for the BBC foreign service. These showed something of her emotional and financial distress after the party cut her Fleet Street connections, and a good deal about her combativeness with the kind of bureaucracy George Orwell aped in *1984* following his Ministry of Information experience during the war. I discovered Charlotte's letters to her agent, Charles Prentice, in the publisher's archives at the University of Reading and in the New York Public Library. At the Museum of the History of Science, which even the taxi man who drove me from the Oxford train station and had been driving in that city for thirty years had never heard of, I found papers from the Science News Service that Charlotte had set up in 1925 to publish JBS's articles.

At the time most of the scientific academic community considered itself above explaining discoveries to the layman and rarely set them down in everyday language. But JBS, who was something of a show-off and cared little about what anyone else thought of him, enjoyed sharing experimental knowledge, and Charlotte knew the market for journalism. So very soon after they fell in love they teamed up professionally. Through the news service she modulated the attitudes of both scientists and the press, and her fluency in French and German put her in the optimal position to draw on and market articles about European as well as British scientific research. Her early releases covered a variety of topics – German discoveries about bees, the Canadian success with insulin, a new British drug that was supposed to speed the healing of broken bones, the telepathic research being done at the universities of Gröningen and Harvard, and JBS's own work. Within two years she'd made him a legend and doubled his income.

In their marriage, the years of which JBS said were among the happiest of his life, the Haldanes had gone their own ways. The early years were good ones for Charlotte too, and productive ones. Aside from her journalism she wrote several novels – *Man's World* (1926) was a model for Aldous Huxley's *Brave New World* (1932) – and a book about motherhood, which brought wide public debate. In Cambridge she became even more famous for her parties at Robuck, the Haldanes' large Victorian house beside the river. JBS called her gatherings "Chatty's Addled Salon." Whoever was there on an afternoon would find Martin Case, one of his old students who lived in the house and was Charlotte's lover, playing jazz on her Bechstein grand. In 1930 she dedicated *Brother to Bert* to him. Like JBS, Charlotte was a freethinker, a marvellous antidote to academic Cambridge, and she supplied plenty of good food and drink. Among her other salon regulars were William Empson, Michael Redgrave, Hugh Sykes-Davies, John Davenport, Jack Cowan, Robert Lazarus, and Malcolm Lowry. Lowry figured in her 1932 novel, *I Bring Not Peace*, which she dedicated to him and where she christened his legend of himself in print.

Gordon Bowker had just published his biography of Lowry, *Pursued by Furies* (1993), when I met him. After dinner in a Greek restaurant near his Notting Hill house he took me home to show me a short video of Charlotte talking about Lowry. Gordon was a prize-winning biographer of Orwell and Joyce as well, and he must have known from our conversation that I needed to see the tape because he insisted I go with him despite the midnight hour. On his small TV screen Charlotte sat in a rocking chair and talked, not with the high-pitched insistency people who'd known her had described, but in a controlled voice and with a very polished upper-class accent. It played havoc with my impression of her. That picture of her rocking back and forth gently, her white hair pulled back, her hands arthritic, was very different from the one her family had pressed on me of her younger self leaning against the mantel, dry martini in hand, to lecture them about politics before every Sunday lunch. Gordon was right to insist that I needed to hear Charlotte talk and to see her move, however briefly, before I tried to make a coherent narrative of her life.

As Vincent Brome had warned me in the British Library, writing biography is hard work, although these days electronic searches make the job far easier. Before digitization, primary research had to be gathered from distant and often uncatalogued archives and, as with Charlotte, those archives had to be hunted down. I'd be presented with boxes of disordered papers and not allowed to copy anything, or be confronted with old and over-used machines to reproduce even older microfilm or newsprint that was so fragile it often had to be left for the keepers to copy at huge expense.

Then there was the travel. Not the kind Norman Sherry did to his peril walking in Graham Greene's footsteps, or Richard Holmes who, in following Robert Louis Stevenson's journey in the Cévennes, came to believe he actually saw and met his imaginary subject. I needed critical distance, and the archival research for Charlotte's biography was difficult because my teaching responsibilities meant shuttling back and forth from Montreal to London. Charlotte's books were in the British Museum and her articles in the newspaper collection at Collindale, a long tube ride from Bloomsbury. And there were many return trips from London to Reading and Caversham at the beginning and end of a day's work in the archives there. Back in Montreal I was reliant on inter-library loans because only two of Charlotte's twenty-eight books and translations were in the combined university libraries of the city.

But if electronic searches are easier they also dampen the hunt and, frustrating as the trail often was, I loved following the bread crumbs Charlotte had left. As Virginia Woolf said in *Orlando*, "the first duty of a biographer … is to plod." There were many pleasurable London rambles – up to South Hampstead where Charlotte had lived as a girl, and through Regent's Park to the Haldanes' house at 16 Park Village East where they moved to from Cambridge. Eventually I crossed the city to find 20 Abbey Road in St John's Wood where Charlotte died blind, dictating her last book, *Madame de Maintenon* (1970), to a secretary paid for by the Royal Literary Fund and the National Institute for the Blind. And I was grateful for the friendships I made along the route.

No electronic search could have replaced my dinners with Gordon, and with Ronnie Burghes and his wife, Betty. Ronnie had been one of the first British Battalion volunteers to fight fascism in the Spanish Civil War, and at sixteen one of the youngest. Because of his youth and long legs he had often run information to and from the front lines. At the Battle of Jarama outside Madrid a bullet had gone straight through his left arm, luckily without doing serious damage. His stories bled into Charlotte's and explained how her anti-fascism and motherly concern for him had led her to join the party.

Born two years later than Virginia Woolf, Charlotte was one of the so-called surplus women, women who had outnumbered men in Great Britain for a few decades before she was born, and by the 1921 census by close to 1.75 million. Why should they not emigrate to Canada, Lady Bruton suggested in *Mrs. Dalloway*. "Young people of both sexes, born of respectable parents" should go. But Hugh Whitbread knew Millicent Bruton "exaggerated ... Emigration was not to others the obvious remedy." Not for the men anyway. And whether Charlotte, whose education was stopped by her father's failed business, and whose parentage was German on her father's side and Jewish on both, would have been "respectable" stock in Lady Bruton's mind is doubtful.

In any case, by 1925 when *Mrs. Dalloway* was published, like many women of her age Charlotte had already been making unorthodox domestic arrangements for herself that would encourage her ambition and identity. She'd had an unexpected child and would soon divorce Burghes and marry JBS. And she was using the freedom she was gaining to write hard. Long before it became a feminist cliché that the personal is political, she was turning the personal into political discussion in widely circulated newspaper articles and books. The question for me was not whether she had made the right decisions, but whether it was possible to use her autobiographical novels as fact.

Tempered with her journalism, where Charlotte's feminist ideas were often light years ahead of her time, I soon found the inner experiences of her characters to be an honest and nuanced account of her generation. And the women whose biographies she'd written – pot-boilers she called them out of financial need – were strong and freethinking like herself. She'd fallen from literary history but she'd bravely broken barriers in her desire to forge a new narrative for living, in and out of marriage and motherhood. So I decided to trust her as an emblematic figure of those women whose way had been opened by the First World War, even if her story was complicated, and enriched, by her communist party connection. I thought her political work during the Spanish Civil War well worth recording, along with the trajectory of her political involvement with the British Communist Party, and the period of deep unhappiness and financial insecurity that followed when she was not trusted by her male colleagues to behave in an intellectual rather than an emotional way.

Charlotte said she survived in the rapid-fire, instant-deadline world of Fleet Street because her father had taught her to drink like a man. After a couple of Fitzrovia pub crawls to trace the Robuck set's hangouts when they graduated from Cambridge, I appreciated her ability. But it was Charlotte's family who helped me through the writing of her biography, along with the honesty of the many other people I met whose anti-fascism had also led them to the communist party during the thirties. And there was Michael Bott at the University of Reading's manuscript library. Michael turned out to be even more indispensable when I edited the correspondence of Leonard Woolf and Trekkie Ritchie Parsons, whose dust jackets he found for me hidden among the various publishers' files he curated.

6

Vincent Brome

Book or Thesis?

One morning in the late seventies I ran into my Dawson colleague Elaine Bander in the old British Library. A fine Jane Austen scholar, she had been working there for several months and had met a group of people who ate daily in the School of Tropical Medicine canteen on Keppel Street. Would I join them? As she led me through the back of the Reading Room and the labyrinthine corridors around the North Library to leave the British Museum by its door on Montague Place, she told me the table was presided over by Vincent Brome, who called himself a journeyman of letters and if asked would say he'd been educated in the North Library. In fact, he was one of the last writers in Britain to have earned an independent living by his pen for fifty years before the days of large advances. His strict rule was that no anecdotal evidence must enter the conversation.

I was placed beside Vincent, who began immediately to display his intellect as a peacock would his feathers. Although he was said to have bedded more women than anyone cared to count, I found him physically unappealing. He was about five foot seven, his hair was auburn, his complexion lightly freckled, and he was so slight of frame I could have lifted him off his feet. As he cut ravenously into his fish an arthritic index finger stuck out above his knife, while from his mouth flowed a fully printable argument on the acceptability of incest. He had been writing about psychoanalysis and analytical psychology, producing among many other books *Freud and His Early Circle* (1967). On his desk in the North Library were the proofs of *Jung, Man and Myth* (1978), the introduction for *Havelock Ellis, Philosopher of Sex* (1981), and an untidy pile of papers filled with scribbled notes and letters for *Ernest Jones: Freud's Alter Ego* (1982). He said that biographies were his bread and butter but at the moment he was writing a novel with a psychological bent. Were his analyses of incest brave? Or was he up to mischief?

As Vincent became one of our closest friends – *The Independent* in 2004 asking me to write his obituary for them – I now know it was a bit of both. The ensuing debate was intellectually vigorous, competitive although never vituperative, tempered with irony and laughter, and not entirely without personal anecdote. I added little to it that day but must have given good audience. On the walk back to the Reading Room Vincent slipped his arm through mine and invited me to join his lunch table anytime. And yes, I could bring my husband.

✪✪✪

"Book or thesis?" Vincent would ask new scholars as they waited in line for their books in the Reading Room. It was the same question Phil Stratford had asked me the day he suggested I write about Graham Greene. If the response Vincent got was as genial as his question, he offered research and publishing advice, and extended an invitation to the Tropical Medicine canteen. As I had learned when I met him there, the meal was unimportant. It was the cross-fertilization of ideas that fuelled the afternoon's work, and the constant friendship that made Vincent's table a kind of club. When Alan and I became regulars the others were philosopher Sue Wilsmore, art historian and curator Hardy George, Diana Manuel, who taught medical students at University College London through the Wellcome Institute, and scientist Michael Moody. But Vincent's table was a movable feast which often included well-established writers too. We met philosophers Ted Honderich and Freddie (A.J.) Ayre there, and Marxist historian Raphael Samuel. When she was in London, Priscilla Meyer, the American scholar of Russian literature, came with her physicist husband, Bill Trousdale, who was also a painter. Sometimes historian Joanna Bourke joined us, and when she was writing Aphra Behn's biography Angeline Goreau was there every day. Canadian-born Italian Renaissance scholar Carol Kidwell came as well. She read Latin faster than I read English and had a Canadian mountain named after her.

And there were irregulars. I remember a southern American professor who came to London annually for two weeks "for the language," which I took to mean that like Henry James he was inhaling the old world. One noon in the mid-1990s an early-middle-aged Japanese professor stood by the door watching us, clearly begging an invitation to the noisy table which by then had relocated to the cafeteria in Senate House. Having spoken to him briefly the day before, Vincent shunned him. But a couple of the regulars argued his loneliness and Vincent relented.

That winter Alan was writing about Anthony Trollope and I was still working on Charlotte Haldane's biography. She and JBS had lived in Park Village East, not far from H.G. Wells's great Palladian house at 13 Hanover Terrace. Glorifying the mechanical, Wells had often gone onto his roof to watch the bombing of London. Vincent said that once when he was interviewing Wells toward his first literary biography a big raid started up, the ack-ack guns on Primrose Hill in full blossom. Vincent was on his way down to Wells's cellar when the old man grabbed him by the arm and made for the roof. There they beheld London ablaze, the bombs going off all around. As Vincent shook, Wells danced about in ecstasy shouting, "Look at it! Isn't it fantastic. And just think – I predicted it all!"

To our astonishment, the silent Japanese professor suddenly spoke. He didn't know that London had been bombed in the war. "How is that possible?" Vincent grimaced and rose to the occasion with a story about the Café de Paris. It was considered the safest restaurant in the city because its dance floor was below ground in what had centuries before been a bear pit. But the floor of the cinema above it was flimsy and the cinema itself had a roof of glass. One night two bombs fell right through the glass and the cinema floor, and exploded in the confined café below. At the time Vincent was writing war propaganda for the Ministry of Information, which had then been in the basement of Senate House where we were having lunch on the fourth floor. When his team got to the bomb site, an RAF Flying Officer, who said he had been rendered semi-conscious by what was an appalling pressure on his head, was bellowing commands.

At one table Vincent saw four people sitting upright. They looked fine until a fireman tapped the uniformed colonel gently on the shoulder and the old man fell stiffly forward on his face. They had all been killed by the bomb without visible injury, their laughs, raised eyebrows, and smiles from before the blast unchanged. "We saw things like that all the time and our accounts were broadcast almost every day on the BBC World Service," Vincent said with an accusatory look at the Japanese professor.

For the next hour the fellow got a detailed lecture on the destruction of London, which ended with an instructive story of British courage. Vincent had been sent to talk to an old woman who'd been partially buried for twenty-four hours in her cellar somewhere near Bethnal Green. When he got there the doctor said she was all right but couldn't be freed for another hour. As Vincent noticed a full bottle of brandy close to her hand he suggested she take a nip. "On no," she replied, "I'm keeping that for an emergency."

✿✿✿

Born on Bastille Day in 1910 to a lower-middle-class Streatham family, Vincent had written hundreds of articles, several plays, and over thirty novels, biographies, and historical studies by the time Alan and I got to know him. For years he had kept his age out of *Who's Who* because he knew publishers preferred the young and he warned me early on that age is an even worse enemy of women writers. In her 1997 farewell to the Round Room, Margaret Drabble speculated that its air had preserved him because he still looked about sixty.

Vincent said that 38 Dahomey Road had been commonplace and comfortable but his parents fought interminably. His father worked in the legal department of an American canning firm. He was thrifty and authoritative and Vincent regarded him as the enemy. He thought his mother silly. When he was alone with her she would push aside the dining table and whirl him around to Viennese waltzes as if she were in a ballroom with chandeliers and a full orchestra. He said she lived for pretty clothes and dancing and when problems arose she made a cup of tea. This was what he speculated she had done decades later when she returned from shopping to find his father on the kitchen floor. She made a cup of tea. Then, realizing her husband must have had a heart attack, she telephoned for the doctor without turning off the gas. At the inquest their deaths were recorded as accidental.

Even as a child Vincent had written stories. A crisis arose when he published two installments of "The Sign of the Golden Cross" in his Streatham Grammar School magazine and the third was disallowed because it was thought too good for a boy to have written. His father accused him of speaking in sentences as though they were manufactured, and didn't want a writer for a son. So at sixteen Vincent was sent to work in a tea broker's office. He stayed only until he figured he had enough money in his pocket to survive for a month, and then defied his father and followed the direction of his hero H.G. Wells. In a rented room on Bernard Street in Bloomsbury he began what he called "the great experiment."

He lived on the breakfast his rent provided and a late lunch of sausages and mash. In the morning he wrote for two hours and in the afternoon for three, quickly producing two overly dramatized autobiographical stories that brought no commercial response. The rest of the time he walked, usually south through Holborn and the dark streets east of Chancery Lane, over to St Paul's Churchyard, and then back along Fleet Street looking for someone to talk to. By March his money was so short that he cut breakfast to reduce his rent, and lived off the late lunch and a midnight cup of coffee he took in a greasy café next to the Russell Square tube station. When a few months later an acceptance arrived from *20-Story Magazine* with a cheque for ten guineas, and the morning after another for 7s 6d for two hundred words he had sent to the "Miscellany" column of the *Manchester Guardian*, he could hardly believe his luck.

20-Story Magazine was edited by Harry Leggett. Vincent described him as a burly man with one blind eye who had been a leader writer on the *Economist* before moving to this pulpy-looking periodical that boasted adventure and mystery stories by Edgar Wallace, Agatha Christie, and Ethel Mannin. In the thirties he wrote several successful novels along with *The Idea of Fiction*. "Know your limitations," Leggett advised when they met and he held out the promise of 50 guineas for a second story of ten thousand words.

When Vincent returned with his typescript Leggett asked if he could make a few adjustments and polished the story with such skill that the raw adolescent wondered if he could ever match it. Then, over an expensive lunch at Scott's, a deal was struck. Vincent would write one story a month after discussing its theme, central idea, and characters with his new mentor. It was in essence a first-rate apprenticeship.

And Leggett offered more. He introduced Vincent to bohemian life and the British Museum Reading Room, where he insisted Vincent read systematically by picking several books on one subject in sequence and then looking for cross-references. Vincent had already read most of Wells and George Bernard Shaw. Leggett introduced him to Bertrand Russell, J.B.S. Haldane, Julian Huxley, and Sigmund Freud. Although he did not lean politically left himself, to Vincent's many questions about the social inequalities of Britain, he encouraged contact with the Fabian Society where Vincent was befriended by Hugh Gaitskill, Ian Mikardo, Roy Jenkins, and Michael Young. The latter two became lifelong friends.

By the end of the twenties Vincent's political and, to a large extent, literary conscience was formed, and perhaps his later penchant for helping those of us in need of publishing advice. "The Library became my life," he said. "I educated myself there and I did all my writing there." As the decades passed he acted as a mentor to scholars he befriended, largely academics for whom he had an autodidact's reverence. As a member of the British Library's Advisory Committee from 1974 when architects Sandy (Colin St John) Wilson and his wife, Mary Jane Long, were asked to assess the Euston Road site for the new building, Vincent vigorously supported moving the Reading Room and the library's great collection of books against the wishes of many irate readers, including everyone at his lunch table. He insisted the books were more important than their readers. We argued that to leave that domed paradise would be like the end of a long love affair.

Vincent was right. And so were we. When the move came in 1997 it ended his life's routine. "The last party in the Reading Room was terrible," he said, "but nostalgia wasn't a good thing to make a judgment from." When he was not strong enough to walk the extra half-mile every day to the new library from his top-floor Queen Anne flat at 45 Great Ormond Street where he'd lived for decades, I often took sandwiches to him for lunch. He wanted me to write his biography but perhaps the fact that I also brought a tape recorder meant I knew I never would.

Tape 1 begins: "I record my Grub Street stories for anyone stupid enough to pick up a pen." As a boy he had wanted to be a scientist, he said. He "had the flamboyant and ridiculous ambition to make a new interpretation of the world." But lack of funds kept him from university and forced him to write, first journalism and stories. Before he wrote the biographies he was best known for he had contributed to almost all of London's leading newspapers and journals. His novels came later. He said that in them he had "wanted to explore an idea that would minimally advance our understanding of ourselves. Their early themes arose in the Fabian Society and the Labour Party. Then they became more psychological." *The Surgeon* (1967) and *The Embassy* (1972) were bestsellers throughout the world. Laurence Olivier had lined up money and a script-writer to turn *The Embassy* into a film because he wanted to play the Ambassador. But he insisted the story be reset in Paris, and Vincent said he "stupidly demanded that it had to take place in a communist country. So the plan fell apart. A couple of plays were produced but nothing was ever filmed and that's where the money is. The novels never made much," he said, "and I now think they weren't very good, although they've all been recently republished. I was really interested in ideas and tried to fit the characters into them."

He didn't always want to write biography but those books brought small advances, and contracts for the novels. The first were *Clement Attlee* (1947), *H.G. Wells* (1951), and *Aneurin Bevan* (1953). *Freud and His Early Circle* began the series about analytical psychology that he was working on when Alan and I met him. After Carl Jung, Havelock Ellis, and Ernest Jones, he circled back to literature, to *J.B. Priestley* (1988) and *The Other Pepys* (1992). "These days biographies are more popular than novels, and easier to sell," he said. "To do a really good one takes years, decades sometimes, so they're now most often written by academics with grants. I had to work faster. I produced a book almost every year until close to the end of the century. But even at that gruelling pace I lived hand to mouth."

On those lunch tapes Vincent talked about his days with Thomas Mann, Jean-Paul Sartre, and Simone de Beauvoir. He'd spent a week with Dorothy Richardson when he was researching his biography of Wells. She was seventy-seven at the time, "had a pile of yellowy hair, and wore a shawl clasped tightly around her short knitted skirt." He said it was dark and blustery when he arrived at her house above the sea in Cornwall and he watched her through the window before he knocked. "She paced up and down with almost military precision, every so often seeming to speak to someone above her." He later learned that her dead husband, Alan Odle, had been over six feet tall.

He said that although her powers were failing there was no questioning them. She was still writing *Pilgrimage* (1938), which May Sinclair called a stream of consciousness before the term got attached to James Joyce and Virginia Woolf. When Vincent saw her, Richardson wrote only a few sentences a week because each paragraph had become such a complex aesthetic problem. Even when he told me this he was still in awe of her.

He'd spent several days with Bertrand Russell who, among other stories, recalled a 1948 plane crash he'd been in en route to Denmark. Since Russell was a heavy pipe smoker he'd told his secretary to make sure he had a seat in the smoking compartment or he'd die. He was wearing heavy boots and a winter overcoat and was still smoking his pipe when he watched the water come into the cabin and felt the tail of the plane sink. Then, as he climbed to the exit door and jumped out, he remembered some advice his Uncle Bertie had given him: "When in trouble in a rough sea, do the breast stroke." He did and was saved by a Danish lifeboat while three other passengers drowned. At the end of this story Vincent mimicked Russell as saying in "a grating, ironical and detached" voice: "If you recall my words – I shall die if I do not get a seat in the smoking compartment – you will see that we have here a very interesting example of a well-known and somewhat common phenomenon, that of telling the truth without knowing it."

My favourite story on the lunch tapes was about Graham Greene. Vincent met him long before I did, just after *The Fallen Idol* and *The Third Man* had brought celebrity. He said he'd turned up at the Albany one April morning at eleven as arranged, to find Catherine Walston stretched out on Graham's sofa wearing little and drinking brandy. He knew her Labour MP husband, Henry Walston, pretty well and had met Catherine several times. Graham said he'd forgotten Vincent was coming to interview him and, as Walston showed no sign of recognizing him, Vincent played her game. He and Graham talked briefly about Hazlitt and about drama. But when he asked Graham about his new novel, Walston answered Vincent's questions as though she were writing the book. She then turned abruptly to Graham and said, "Why don't you get rid of him so we can go back to bed." The novel was *The End of the Affair*, dedicated "To Catherine, with love" in the American edition, in Britain only to "C" because Harry Walston objected. As he showed Vincent out, Graham made a point of telling him that *The End of the Affair* was "the great sex novel."

✪✪✪

Vincent's influence on our London lives was large. Alan and I often went with him to the Savile Club for dinner, and I more often when I was alone in London on my hurried research trips. We also went with him to openings at the Gimpel Fils gallery on Davies Street. It was then run on a daily basis by Kay Moore who, like Alan, had grown up in Winnipeg. She'd won the French Prize for her year at the University of Manitoba and gone to the Sorbonne to study, and then worked at the British Embassy in Paris until May 1940, when she was moved to London with the rest of the staff. There she lived with Alison Grant, who would become Michael Ignatieff's mother, he becoming Kay's godson. Both women were involved with the Special Operations Executive, Kay eventually as head of Air Liaison and the person logistically responsible for sending men and material into occupied Europe, down to the precise landing spot in the targeted field.

Her husband, Ernest Gimpel, or Charles, the SOE codename he kept for life, had joined a French tank regiment in the war, been evacuated from Dunkirk, and then returned to France with the Resistance. He was soon arrested by the Germans. He escaped and returned to France in November 1943, was captured again, tortured by the Gestapo, and sent successively to Buchenwald, Auschwitz, and Flossenburg. According to family lore, his first words when he was released from Flossenburg on 24 April 1945 were, "Where is Kay Moore?"

Vincent said Kay had saved the family's art business from the fluctuations of the British pound and American dollar by insisting that all business be done in Swiss francs. She kept a card index at her side and wrote notes about clients and interested people so that when someone rang or walked in she seemed to remember them intimately. This was invariably welcoming, as in May 2001 when I was on my own in London and rang her up. Her sons were giving a party for her at the gallery that evening, she said. "I'm so glad you're here. I was just addressing your invitation."

Alan and I sometimes dined with Kay at her small house in Stanhope Mews East. Charles had died in 1973 after a successful career as a photographer of the Canadian Arctic, and Kay now shared the house with Bridgit Ferry, who had come to London from Ireland with the Gimpels after the war. One day when I was there alone and Kay had pneumonia, the instant Bridgie went to the kitchen to make us coffee Kay took a half-smoked cigarette from her voluminous smock, quickly inhaled a few puffs and returned it to her pocket before Bridgie came back. "Don't say a word," she cautioned severely, "or you'll never be invited again."

✪✪✪

Kay's brother-in-law Jean Gimpel and his wife, Catherine, held a salon on six winter Sundays every year at their flat on the Chelsea Embankment. They were vibrant parties full of not-so-whispered gossip and competitive witticisms that were frequented by freethinking scientists, doctors, historians, writers, publishers, artists and of course, by Vincent. Jean always talked enthusiastically about medieval technology and his agricultural inventions for Africa that people could repair for themselves and use without gasoline or electricity. On display was a model he'd made for lifting water along with his often humourous drawings that instructed rural villages in India how not to do things, such as bringing animals too close to wells.

Vincent was a womanizer, and at the salon was usually chatting up a female he'd cornered. He had once come up behind me in the library and whispered, "My dear, let's go to my flat for the afternoon." I was only marginally surprised because he flirted his way around the Reading Room regularly. "And if I do, will you have lunch with Alan tomorrow?" I shot back. He was silent for only a moment. "Well maybe not tomorrow, but the next day."

Both in life and print he was always straightforward about sex. He called himself a serial monogamist and shared his life with many talented women including the prize-winning Canadian biographer Phyllis Grosskurth, whose letters tell of an excitement with him unlike any she'd experienced. She gave him up after several years and returned to Ottawa with her husband and two children. For a while she continued to write him about the provincialism of her new life compared with the exuberance she had shared with him in literary London. But Vincent was unmentioned in her autobiography, an omission that infuriated him.

He said he had learned not to ask women about their affairs because when he did they would tell him the man was wonderful and they respected him and nothing more. If, however, he turned as he was leaving and added, "Oh, by the way, I've heard that he loved you," they would say, "Yes, he loved me" and tell him everything. But when he showed me Phyllis Grosskurth's letters he told me not to ask her about their affair if I wrote his biography because she'd stop publication of the book. He then gave me her letters to him in case she challenged me.

Another evening at the salon Vincent left his corner of women and came to lead us hurriedly into the conservatory at the back of the flat to make what he insisted was "an important introduction." And there was Margaret Ann, Lady Elton to Vincent, who watched in utter astonishment as she and Alan fell into each other's arms. Alan and his first wife, Margaret Ann, hadn't seen each other since the John Grierson Conference at McGill in October 1981 when she, Forsyth Hardy, and several of the early British documentary film makers in attendance had come to Richelieu Place for dinner. Basil Wright had brought his tall elegant friend Kassim, who asked if he could help. When Margaret Ann told me to "just say yes," I did, and without instruction Kassim finished cooking dinner, served and ate it while adding to the conversation, and then cleaned up, leaving not a fork out of place.

Arthur Elton had died in 1973 and when Margaret Ann died in 1995 we got to know their children, Julia, Rebecca, and Charles. We spent a weekend with Julia and her partner, the great structural engineer Frank Newby, at Clevedon Court. On Sunday we went to All Saint's Church where Julia, a wonderful musician and a leading authority on the history of British engineering, sang in the choir while Frank, Alan, and I sat up straight in the third pew. Knowing Alan to be an atheist but a lover of the liturgy, Julia had provided him with an ancient copy of Thomas Cranmer's *Book of Common Prayer* from the Clevedon Court library. As he shuffled the pages the man standing behind him leaned over and replaced the book, whispering rather insistently, "This is what we use now." At the end of the service when we were told by the vicar to hug one another, a young fellow with gnarled hands and a too small suit in the pew in front of us turned and kissed me on the lips. He said his name was Robert. Could he show me around the graveyard? I thought he was straight out of Thomas Hardy. Alan and Frank said he was looking for a longer kiss behind a tombstone. As we drank sherry before lunch in front of an enormous fire in the beautiful fourteenth-century Great Hall at Clevedon I thought how wonderful England was, and how little it had changed.

✿✿✿

H.G. Wells had been a god to Vincent since childhood. They'd met in Regent's Park one September morning in 1941 when Wells released himself from the clutches of two grandchildren and plopped down heavily on a bench. The great man was in his seventies and unwell. Vincent approached him. "You *are* H.G. Wells aren't you?" The answer came "like a high-pitched squeal of chalk going across a slate," Vincent remembered. "Who else looks quite so palsied and decayed?" When he told me this, I thought of Virginia Woolf, who wrote in *A Room of One's Own* about seeing "a bent figure" one October evening in Cambridge "formidable yet humble, with her great forehead and her shabby dress." Unlike Vincent, who took the male prerogative and interrupted Wells, Woolf had left the great classical scholar Jane Harrison to her thoughts.

The following spring Vincent took up Wells's invitation to his house overlooking Regent's Park. He found the old man sitting outside under his Panama hat and behind dark glasses with a notebook on his lap recording the symptoms of his ill health. "So you want to be a writer," Wells said. "What a mistake." His advice was to find £30,000 so Vincent could be free to speak his mind. When asked where to find it, Wells advised "robbery, the stock exchange, pornography. It doesn't matter how you get it," he said. "Most people with £30,000 have robbed other people."

Soon afterward, Vincent met his other hero, George Bernard Shaw, and was peppered with questions. "No education? Marvellous. Ambition? It has to be large." When Vincent said he wanted to be a writer Shaw listed his own year's work – he was eighty-seven at the time – then roared, "And you hope to compete with that, do you?" Vincent admitted to collecting material toward a biography of Wells, and Shaw bellowed: "You must be madder than I thought. No one will ever contain HG between the covers of a book. Wait till he hears of this. He'll bring the house down round you."

Wells didn't but his son Gip tried to in February 1951 after Vincent's biography had been recommended by the Book Society and its publication date set for mid-month with Longmans, Green. Wells père had died in 1946 before the book was begun, so Vincent sent the manuscript to Gip and assured him that anything offensive or inaccurate would be removed. Wells fils said simply that Vincent must face the reviews and arranged at the Savile, where Vincent was up for membership, that at least the first of them would be negative. He told

Desmond MacCarthy he would resign if Vincent were taken into the Club, and then invited a group of critics there for dinner and pronounced Vincent's biography piratical. When MacCarthy's review in the *Sunday Times* trashed the book, Compton Mackenzie, who was on the Book Society selection committee along with V.S. Pritchett and Edmund Blunden, phoned Vincent to say he didn't think MacCarthy had read it. He would write a review himself. It appeared the following week in the *Observer* praising Vincent. With MacCarthy's review the *Sunday Express* had cancelled the biography's serialization; with MacKenzie's it was reinstated.

Vincent told me this as a directive about how reviews are assigned and controlled after *The Dangerous Edge* had gone to the publisher. I was reminded of the afternoon he came excitedly into the Reading Room holding up a terrific review of his *J.B. Priestley* and exclaimed, "I don't even know the man who wrote it!" About my *Dangerous Edge*, he added financial facts to further prepare me. For *H.G. Wells* he'd had a £250 advance of which his agent had taken 10 per cent. He had paid his typist £50; another £50 had gone to income tax. Longmans, who to their credit had refused to abandon him to MacCarthy's initial review by fighting back with ads and an agreement to take two more of his books, had made £250,000 profit that year. Vincent estimated their chief editor would have been paid about £1500 a year. For his own eighteen months' work he figured he'd earned £125, beefed up considerably by the book's serialization, which had brought an unexpected £2000. "What a lashing they gave me," he said. "It was my first literary biography and before Mackenzie rang me I nearly killed myself. A few years later, Gip Wells told me he'd over reacted and when he finally read the book decided it was a good rendition of his father. And don't forget," Vincent cautioned, "few books get serialized."

To update his point he said that in the late 1980s he'd been paid a £30,000 advance against royalties and serialization in the *Sunday Times* for his 800-page *J.B. Priestley* (1988), which took him three years to write. And he'd had the headache of having to move to Hamish Hamilton when Macmillan demanded two sets of corrections he refused to make. "You don't get anything," he said, "and your book vanishes off the shelves in a year." He showed me a recent clipping he'd saved from *The Times* about the number of writers in England having been reduced because of their financial circumstances from three thousand in 1982 to thirteen hundred by the end of the decade. One earned about £750,000 and most of the others made under £1500 a year. And he warned that writers' circumstances were continuing to decline. He was proven right. The British Authors' Licensing and Collecting Society recently reported that in 2022 the median annual earnings from self-employed writing, which include genres Vincent had no access to like writing for games, are now £7000. My earnings from *The Dangerous Edge* came nowhere near even Vincent's minimal calculations. But the reviews it got were positive and I had a teaching job in Montreal and a research grant to pay my bills. Nonetheless, these were sobering facts, the more so since Vincent and Graham both believed teaching required too much creative energy and provided too little intellectual stimulation. On that last point I disagreed.

❂❂❂

At Vincent's ninetieth birthday lunch on Bastille Day in 2000 his friends gathered at the Savile and brought their new books for him, a birthday tradition. They were displayed on a table at the side of the room. Michael Young, now Baron Young of Dartington, spoke about his long friendship with Vincent, about his books, and about the dreams they'd had for the world after the war. He was modest about his own contribution to the political life of Britain and to the advancement of socialist thought. Sue Wilsmore, Catherine Gimpel, and I were the only women around that very large table of men. Sue and I had picked Vincent up at his flat on Great Ormond Street. We'd forced him to change his socks because one was blue and the other brown. He thought our insistence that they match a bourgeois affectation, and the delay made him nervous about being late for his party. When the driver tried to jolly him Vincent told the fellow to shut up.

He was often abrupt with stupidity but this rudeness reflected his insecurity at the thought of not arriving in time to greet his guests. Only once before had I seen him so agitated. In March 1992 he had wanted to come with me to Church House at Westminster Abbey when, just after Graham died, PEN International had invited me to talk about working with him. Alan and I never attended each other's public events and I was far too nervous and felt too inadequate to the task to take Vincent myself. Instead of socializing with London's literati before the talk as I would have needed to had he been with me, I spent half an hour walking back and forth on Westminster Bridge reciting Wordsworth's eponymous "Ode" to calm down. As W.H. Auden once said about himself, I felt like a provincial clergyman shuffling into a room full of dukes.

My talk went well. And so did Vincent's party. Once we got to the Savile he was his usual charming self. He matched Michael Young's admiration of him with an account of Michael's enormous accomplishments and of their quick and deep friendship, and he thanked everyone for having written the many books on the side table.

I last saw Vincent a few days before his death in 2004. He could see and hear little by then and for a couple of months had been unable to flee into one of his beloved Bloomsbury squares to distance himself from his uncontrollable novelist's mind. I had just flown in from Montreal but Alan and I had listened on the phone for several weeks to his helplessness in the face of the unstoppable, his anger, his fear, his tears. He was at the Middlesex Hospital in a large room which also held the nurse's desk. Close by was a man chained to his bed. The nurses said he was a murderer who had been brought sick from jail and he moved under his sheet with the sound of Marley's ghost. Vincent had often argued that "if we believe in birth control, then why not death control." But euthanasia was still illegal and the barbiturates he'd stocked were far outdated. I don't think he'd have taken them anyway. He wanted too much to keep recording his world even as he fell away from it. He was in a drugged sleep when I arrived and I sat quietly holding his hand until the rattling chain summoned him back to his imminent death. "What are you thinking?" I asked. He must have mistaken what I said because he responded decisively: "Of course I'm thinking. That's what we're here for."

7

Leonard Woolf and Trekkie Ritchie Parsons

Their Love Letters

I was told to meet Elizabeth Ingles, the curator of the Leonard Woolf Archive at the University of Sussex, at nine o'clock on Wednesday, 28 May 1997. It was drizzling and foggy. As the train to nearby Falmer was scheduled to arrive either forty-five minutes earlier or an hour later, Bet found me waiting on the very damp steps of the library when she came to work. With her Scottish directness she asked many questions. Since she had only recently opened Trekkie Ritchie Parsons and Leonard Woolf's correspondence, how had I heard about it? Why did I want to read it? Did I understand that I could copy nothing?

Dropping names helped a little. Trekkie had given the writer Jeanne MacKenzie the correspondence, leaving her free to do whatever she wanted with it. But Jeanne had died and Trekkie had then sealed the letters until her own death and deposited them at the University of Sussex. I had met Jeanne and her husband, Norman, in Montreal at a dinner party hosted by Tobie and Herb Steinhouse. There I learned about Leonard's love for Trekkie, and that she had lived with him half the week for the better part of twenty-six years and the other half with her husband, Ian Parsons, the head of Chatto & Windus. Bet knew Jeanne's daughter, Julia, had heard of the Rudés, and said Trekkie had had close friends in Rye. I had permission to read the letters, but Bet had been Trekkie's friend and was trying to protect her, as I soon discovered many people were.

She led me into a long narrow room with a door at either end and seated me at a table with a glass wall behind it. Outside was a small enclosed garden across which was a similar glass wall. She piled the boxes of Leonard's letters on one side of the table, Trekkie's on the other. Seeing my pencil she said, "Oh, you've worked with manuscripts before," and then added insistently what she had told me in her office, that I must not copy anything. As I had only one paper under my pencil she agreed that I could take a few notes and left. It was past ten by then and I had until five o'clock. I opened both sets of boxes and, matching the dates, began to read the letters as a correspondence.

About ten minutes later Bet came through the door to my left. Did I need anything? She exited right, and very soon re-entered left. After another sally I was so absorbed I didn't realize she was back until she stopped abruptly in front of the table. "Oh, you like them!" I was as astonished by her remark as she seemed to be. She didn't come back and I didn't leave my chair until five when I went to find her downstairs with students.

The letters had left me struck for words and when Bet saw me all I could say was, "Thank you. Thank you for today." As I turned to go she asked what I planned to do. I had wanted to write Trekkie's biography but now thought that the correspondence should speak for itself, that it should be published in its entirety. I thanked her again and when I turned to leave a second time she said, "I think you'll be hearing from me." She rang the next day. Of the three copyright holders, she said Sheila Dickinson was the most important. She lived in Rye. If I were to ring her at nine that evening she might talk to me. Sheila agreed to a visit on Saturday and from then on I followed Bet's sage suggestions exactly.

Sheila was suffering terribly with arthritis. She lived in a beautiful tall house on the sea side of Church Square where the wind blew through the top-floor cracks and windows into the room that had been her husband's study. I had walked from Cadborough Cliff carrying one yellow rose from Doreen's garden. We made a pot of tea together. I placed the milk and cups on the tray and carried it for Sheila into the drawing room. We talked about her poet husband, Patric Dickinson, who had died in 1994. He'd been poetry editor for the BBC and Gresham Professor at City University. He was a fine golfer, a Cambridge Blue, and he and Trekkie's husband had played together. As Alan was almost a scratch golfer we compared notes about the philosophical geometry of the game. We talked about their children, David and Virginia. Trekkie and Ian were their godparents and the children had often spent holidays with the Parsons. And there were gardens – Sheila's, which she could no longer tend, Alan's and mine in Sutton, Trekkie's and Leonard's, and the "The History of the Strange Stapelia," the botanical article they'd written together in 1945 for the *Geographical Magazine*. We talked about what had been done to Monk's and to Charleston, Vanessa Bell's house, which she had shared with painter Duncan Grant and where her daughter-in-law Olivier Bell now lived.

Trekkie, Sheila told me, was a terrific cook and used many Scottish recipes. But Ian made the mayonnaise, the best ever, and the martinis. Sheila had stories about Juggs Corner, the 1930s house half an hour's walk from Rodmell, which Trekkie and Ian had bought in 1954. They used to dance together so well that everyone else stopped dancing to watch them. They were an elegant couple. Trekkie was outspoken and independent and very private. Sheila knew about Leonard but how much was unclear. She said only that when Trekkie was at Juggs and he rang she'd go immediately to Monk's House. And Ian … he'd had a long affair with Norah Smallwood, who became the head of Chatto & Windus when he retired. Trekkie tolerated her and was jealous of her. She was jealous of Virginia Woolf too, Sheila said. I knew this was untrue.

As the fading afternoon light cast its intimacy across the room, Sheila began slowly but without stopping to tell me about a young woman Patric had loved, a young woman who had come to live with them in Church Square and who, she said almost inaudibly, she too had come to love. "People talked. They thought it all very wrong," she whispered and fell silent. I was deeply moved and didn't break the silence for what must have been a noticeable pause. "I don't think people own one another," I said. Sheila took my hand and in her own time said she'd arrange for me to publish the correspondence. We talked on the phone and wrote to each other over the next three years, but I never saw her again.

Even my quick read of the letters and the concern both Sheila and Bet had for Trekkie made me aware I was onto something very precious. Not because half the correspondence was Leonard's, which made it valuable in itself, but because of the questions Trekkie's life had posed and the decision she'd made to preserve her answers to them in the letters. These days they seem ordinary but they're not simple. Here was a woman born not much later than Charlotte Haldane. They were both avowed feminists. Charlotte had married twice, then gone her own way. Trekkie had married fellow artist Peter Brooker in 1926 when she was at the Slade. With him she'd lived a lean life for a few years in London and country cottages in England and France. She said the marriage had been a mistake from the beginning and that she'd never marry again. Then she met Ian. He had just become a director of Chatto & Windus. She divorced Peter and lived with Ian for a couple of years to see if marriage would work before marrying him. Then she met Leonard, and with courage, ingenuity, and determination imagined a different narrative for the three of them and with their help sustained it. On 2 November 1951 she wrote in her diary: "Until women are women first and wives afterwards 75% of them will be unhappy."

You can't fully perceive another person's experience but it's the biographer's job to get as close to it as you can. The war had occasioned the beginning of Trekkie's domestic arrangement. Why had she made it permanent? Had the war so shaken her confidence that she needed both men in their separate ways to help her rebuild it? How had the juggling of the two men affected her art, and the maintenance of a silence that had been so tight that Leonard had said nothing even to Vanessa? Then there was the question of children. Trekkie had never wanted any and had made it clear to Ian before they married that there would be none. Why then did she take in other people's for weekends and holidays as well as various relatives, her "liabilities" she called them, who also absorbed time when she might have painted?

She was determined to be free but the call of conventional life had clearly remained powerful in her. Was this contradiction between artistic freedom and bourgeois social arrangements what she was trying to work out in her lyrical paintings, and never did to her own satisfaction? She may not have been the female Stanley Spencer of her generation but she was a good painter and her children's books were very good. Perhaps she was not as talented as Leonard had thought her to be. Or did she simply not know how to work the art market, which was what her novelist sister Alice Ritchie thought.

Finding a balance between one's heart and one's professional life still unsettles women, and in Trekkie's day, even with trusted housekeepers and gardeners, it was as hard to achieve. Sheila and her son, David, who scattered Trekkie's ashes on the Downs above Juggs Corner in 1995, were two of the copyright holders of the letters. The third party was the University of Sussex. When their quick permission to publish was given I thought it was because of my books about Graham and especially because of *Reflections*, which had moved me from academic into trade publishing. But I was told it was because of my biography of Charlotte Haldane, of which only a few early copies were then available. If I could make a story of her life they figured I could write Trekkie's. Here was testimony to the seemingly banal questions of talented women's lives. Perhaps everyone's protectiveness spoke to a fear that Trekkie would seem unimportant against the extended Bloomsbury canvas. In *Orlando* Virginia Woolf wrote that "when we are writing the life of a woman we may, it is agreed, waive our demand for action and substitute love instead." However tongue-in-cheek this was meant, before Sheila gave me permission to publish she was certainly afraid that Trekkie would become a footnote in Leonard's story. And she thought readers might condemn Trekkie for how she'd lived.

With the letters was a sealed bundle of legal papers. In them I found a story worthy of François Mauriac. An error had been made by the solicitor when Leonard signed the final copy of his will and, even though proof of error was readily provided, his nephew, Cecil Woolf, had accused Trekkie of "undue influence" in becoming his executrix and residuary legatee, something she had been without knowing it for the previous ten years. In order to prove that no "further particulars would be given after discovery," Trekkie had had to produce her private correspondence with Leonard in probate court, and their relationship had become public copy. She was sixty-nine at the time and never forgot the indignity.

Anneliese West, Trekkie's much loved housekeeper, was the first person after Bet and Sheila to help me. She knew things no one else did. She said that before the court case Ian and Trekkie had burned a lot of paper. That probably accounted for the missing letters. I remembered this when later I got hold of Trekkie's diaries and found that many pages had been torn out. Since I assumed those letters had to do with evidence that might have been detrimental in court, they probably had to do with sex. In order to carry out Leonard's wish to give Monk's House and his papers to the university, Trekkie had to prove Cecil Woolf's charge of "undue influence" wrong so that the magistrate could dismiss their love as "one of those literary and social friendships which are quite remarkable in the history of literature."

I knew that Trekkie had told the Australian critic Peter Alexander that there had been no sex. But Peter had told me he only half believed her. Her close friend Professor Douglas Brewer said she'd told him the same out of the blue and he didn't know why, since he'd never asked. I suggested it was because of the court case. Since Douglas and his wife were involved with Trekkie's legal affairs after Ian died, and with Anneliese's after she in turn died, it was understandable that she remain consistent. Of course there's no way to know, and when I first read the letters it seemed as unimportant to me as it still does whether she and Leonard had slept together. But I soon realized that what Trekkie had told Peter and Douglas was a strong indicator of her character. She was strictly honest, everyone said so. And she was stubborn and loyal. Having slipped Cecil Woolf's noose, in her loyalty to Leonard and to Ian had she defied him again by leaving the letters sealed in the university vault and mentioning to Douglas what she had?

Douglas and Trekkie had been close. In the afternoon I spent with him at his house listening to stories about her and looking at her paintings I realized that he loved her deeply as a friend. He told me she'd been seriously incapacitated with arthritis and eventually unable to paint. She'd had to leave Juggs for a sheltered apartment where she fell and for a time no one had come to rescue her. Douglas had been away and he indicated in broken sentences that when they'd taken her to hospital she'd inveigled someone to pump up the morphine, or done it herself. This upset him because he said her death hadn't been necessary. She'd left her body to medical science. He talked about her intelligence, her outspokenness, her many friendships, sometimes stubbornness, tenacity, talent, warmth, beauty, and humour. We were sitting in his car outside the Lewes train station when he told me she'd said no sex with Leonard. When I said I thought she'd told him this because of the court case, suddenly this self-contained man began to sob. My explanation had meant more than just a provident lie to him. It had meant a break in her trust of him, and I was very sorry for what I'd said.

Anneliese also told me the weekly routine. Trekkie went to London on Monday to attend publishers' events with Ian. From Tuesday to Friday she was with Leonard at Monk's House. Then she went to Juggs Corner. Ian came home from London bearing his dirty laundry. Leonard picked her up Saturday morning to shop in Lewes. She was often not ready and there were loud arguments with Ian who, Anneliese said, had other women as well as Norah Smallwood. When they began to ring him at home Trekkie helped him get rid of them.

She took me up the road from the cottage the Parsons had built for her to the Juggs Corner house, which was then owned by Jennie Yates. It was a beautiful, generous house with a magnificent view over the Downs where Trekkie's ashes had been strewn. Several of her wall paintings were still there. On the door to the stairs a fisherman held a long fish in each hand, and on the walls near the kitchen there were other fish. Did she paint them after her trip in February 1960 to Ceylon with Leonard? She had decorated the fireplace with a brimming jug of roses. In her diary she called painting on walls "a dangerous taste" because it took her away from her serious work. Nonetheless, she enjoyed preparing the space, working in gouache, and then varnishing it over. The "Vases" carpet designed by Duncan Grant and woven by Wilton Royal for Virginia Woolf in 1932 was no longer spread across the living room floor. But the three-inch letters that Ian had scratched on one of the long windows that looked beyond the garden were still there. They marked the visit of the American writer William Humphrey, who had bought his painter wife, Dorothy, a ring with a large stone he was told was a diamond. "Well," Ian had said, "there's one way to be sure," and carved WH & DH into the glass with it.

And Anneliese introduced me to Trekkie's neighbours Nancy Fortescue and Vera Kadden, who were great ornithologists and knew about the garden. They told me that Trekkie had memorized poetry all her life and quoted Dido's "When I am laid in earth" to them the day before she died. Baroness Nora David took me on a tour of the House of Lords and gave me several whiskies as she confirmed that Ian had many girlfriends and told me that he and Trekkie had sniped at each other continually. Trekkie, she said, was much closer to Leonard. Ruth Rendell, who had just been made a peer, happened to be sitting beside us. The story of the letters seemed to interest her and when we walked into the rain together I wondered if it would become fodder for one of her crime novels. Olivier Bell said that Vanessa was pleased about Trekkie because her relationship with Leonard was so easy and harmonious. "She was the exact opposite of Virginia and in no way a substitute. Duncan loved her." The gifted potter Ursula Mommens said Trekkie lived in the present and talked little about her past. Some of her closest friends didn't even know about her wonderful children's books. This I thought strange. "To be hugged by her was to be really hugged," Ursula said. "Her portraits were especially good. She should have had more recognition."

I must have been one of the last people to interview Dadie (George H.W.) Rylands. He was ninety-five. The stairs to his Cambridge rooms at King's College were hung to the ceiling with paintings, several by Duncan Grant and Vanessa Bell. At the top on wall hooks, coats were piled over one another above a heap of shoes. The door was wide open. Inside an enormous and almost empty room I found Dadie sitting alone in his large cushioned window seat looking across the great lawn to the Cam. He had lived in those rooms painted by Dora Carrington and Douglas Davidson most of his life. He sat there like a cherub, very small and beautiful and ethereal. He said his eyes were bad and he was pretty deaf. Would I sit close to him?

Through the next couple of hours he often put his arm around me, his hand sometimes running loosely down my sweater as though he were tracing a person to compensate for his failing sight. He had been a fine critic and one of the best theatre directors of his generation. He talked about Lydia Lopokova and John Maynard Keynes, John Gielgud, Michael Redgrave, Trekkie's close friend Peggy Ashcroft, both Woolfs. He told me about working as a student at the Hogarth Press, about a few of the many plays he'd directed, about recording the whole of the Shakespeare canon, and heading the Arts Theatre after Keynes's death. Finally he came to his sojourns at Juggs Corner with Ian and Trekkie:

> They had blood battles shouting at each other. That never happened with Leonard. No one understands how difficult it was for him with Virginia. He had to be always on guard. He was

very lucky to meet Trekkie. She gave him the best years of his life. After Virginia died he and Trekkie did everything together. I travelled with them sometimes in the car. I toured about with Ian and Trekkie too. We walked in Hardy country together and I took them to Down House where I was born. But Trekkie was more fun when Leonard was there. He was very much in love with her and paid attention to her paintings, which he took seriously. Ian never did. He wasn't interested in painting. Leonard wanted her to show her work to Vanessa and Duncan, who loved her. She was too embarrassed. She was a good painter but distracted by her lithography. That generation was supported by work off the canvas and Trekkie had her jackets and children's books. She thought Virginia got Lili Briscoe wrong in *To the Lighthouse*, that this was not how a painter saw the world, that it was possible to be both an artist and a mother.

Before I could ask why she had then not wanted children we were interrupted by his caregiver, who said he was tired and I must go. "No, no, not yet," he pleaded. But she insisted and Lily Briscoe vanished. In our last few minutes Dadie said, "Everyone wanted to know about Bloomsbury, and the critics made up stories about us. Why couldn't they leave us as we were? We told the truth. We always told the truth. Why couldn't they believe us?" I remembered the self-aggrandizement of the film people I'd interviewed when I wrote about Graham Greene's cinema work and how quickly I'd learned never to believe anyone unless I was told approximately the same thing by three people. I remembered Graham saying he couldn't understand why people didn't see what was in front of them when they called his narrative turf Greeneland. And Sigrun Bülow-Hübe's directive that the detail tells the truth.

At first the innocence of Dadie's question surprised me. But I came to think of it as wise, pointing as it did to the difference between the life lived and the life recorded. The letters were the life recorded as it was being lived, by Trekkie and Leonard for each other's eyes alone.

With the court case, the detail of that private experience had changed and, even in Trekkie's eyes, been influenced by social convention. She'd been forced to read herself, her life lived, the way other people might, and decided to preserve it in the form she wanted, and perhaps needed, it read. One way or another, it was her truth and Dadie's question that firmed my decision to publish all the letters, when clipping them might have been easier.

❂❂❂

The London agent I had was enthusiastic about the project and told me to keep working, that he'd find a publisher when I was ready. But he never did and after close to a year of contact he wouldn't even say if he'd approached anyone. I learned from one of his partners that he often did nothing and Vincent told me he'd stopped using agents years before after a couple of similar experiences. Chatto & Windus was my first and obvious choice and to my relief Jenny Uglow rang me within a few days of my enquiry. Being one of the finest writers in England, she understood immediately how I wanted the book to read.

There would have to be footnotes with the explanations necessary for an international edition. I wanted them to be a conversational part of the letters and my editorial notes to be part of the story, to say what I did, and why and where I might have been mistaken. Trekkie's spelling was careless and often inventive. She punctuated conversationally if at all. Her handwriting was sometimes illegible because she was in a hurry and didn't put down her lithographer's crayon. I wanted readers to know these vulnerabilities as part of her professional woman's difficulties, her self-doubt, her domestic responsibilities, her lack of time. Because Trekkie was so private few people knew much about her. I had been sent her diaries with copyright to them by a relative in France who'd found them in a trunk from Juggs that he had never opened. I would use them to fill in the time gaps in the letters. And I wanted sexual transparency right at the beginning of my introduction, the question the probate hearing had raised probably being the reason Trekkie had kept the letters at all. If I could shape the book in this way, I thought the correspondence would fall naturally into Trekkie's wider life and read like a story. Letters form a quasi-biography, and I needed to know as much about her as if I were her biographer.

⚙⚙⚙

Born in Durban in 1902, Marjorie Tulip Ritchie had spent her childhood learning about nature from her Aunt Mary (whom she called Fannie) and trekking about collecting botanical specimens to paint – scarlet pea-flowers off the kaffir-boom at the edge of the family paddock, jacaranda blossoms from the swarm of blue above their whitewashed cottage. Her architect father, Alan McGregor Ritchie, had followed his sister there from Scotland and then joined the British Army to fight the Boers. When the World War broke out, he returned to Britain and enlisted as a major in the Royal Artillery. Trekkie and her siblings followed with their mother in 1917. Fannie remained in Durban for another thirty years.

Twenty-two-year-old Alice went to Newnham College, Cambridge; eighteen-year-old Pat joined the Royal Flying Corps. Fifteen-year-old Trekkie finished school in Tunbridge Wells and in the summers went to Scotland to stay with her other aunt, Fuzzells. These formidable Ritchie aunts were prominent in the letters and diaries. Mary had been a leader in the teaching of nature studies in Natal. Her book *The Drama of the Year in South Africa* was clearly the model for Trekkie's hugely successful nature study series, *Come and See*. Leonard was fond of her and she often stayed with Trekkie at Monk's after she retired. Leonard shared her colonial interests and appreciated her extensive botanical knowledge.

No one knew Fuzzells's real name, only that she had been a teacher in Scotland. In desperation one day I sent a plea for help addressed literally to the Department of Education, Edinburgh. Very soon I was telephoned by an excited woman who said, "This is the most interesting query we've ever had." Fuzzells was Elizabeth Ida Ritchie and she had lived near Balerno in the outskirts of Edinburgh in a house called The Glen. It had been built as a flax mill in 1905, then converted to a grain mill that had burned inside. She'd bought it in 1921 and rebuilt it to live in the lower part while her students and former girls from Tynecastle School in Edinburgh used the upper floor as a dormitory. All this came over the phone along with the name of the present owners and permission to ring them.

Trekkie said Fuzzells would have been a notable reformer of education had she not taken so close a personal view of things and lived with her little company of disciples. To me she sounded a humourless spiritualist who demanded loyalty to herself and her routine of children's parties and the jumble sales that raised money for the Tynecastle child garden and nursery she'd founded in 1929. She often irritated Trekkie, who nonetheless considered both aunts to be her responsibility, along with Ian's mother, whom she disliked intensely.

So while Trekkie had her father's and Aunt Fannie's artistic gene, her background was military and Protestant do-gooderly. But unlike the case with so many women of her generation, her father and brother had survived the war. Even sister Alice, who had worked for the League of Nations Secretariat after Cambridge, had written about war in *The Peacemakers* (1928), and her second novel, *Occupied Territory* (1930), was about postwar Germany where their father, by then a colonel, was commanding his regiment. Hogarth Press had published both. It was through Alice that Trekkie had done her first dust jackets for Hogarth in the early thirties, for Alice's *Occupied Territory* (1930), R.M. Fox's *Drifting Men* (1930), John Hampson's popular *Saturday Night at the Greyhound* (1931), and Vita Sackville-West's *All Passion Spent* (1931). They were talented and ambitious sisters with little family money to rely on. Alice seemed never satisfied with her work. Virginia Woolf said she alternately wrote and burned it. And in 1936 Alice told Leonard that Trekkie became depressed when the paintings she'd sent to the Artists of Fame & Promise exhibitions didn't sell.

Then there was war again with its related work for Trekkie and Ian's absences with the RAFVR in France. And Alice's death from cancer at the end of October 1941. Leonard had come to visit her when she was dying in Trekkie's Victoria Square house. From then on he brought Trekkie garden produce from Monk's. In May 1942, when she was ill with repeated bouts of quinsy and flu that eventually left her close to pernicious anaemia, and Ian was away, he keep a close eye on her. By December she was staying with him in Sussex and within the year she and Leonard were deeply in love. When Ian returned permanently in August 1944, they began to set up what I came to call their *ménage à trois à trois ménage.*

To my mind Trekkie's background explained her deep familial loyalty and her anxiety of exile; the Second World War in part her depression, her self-doubt, and certainly her sense of the fragility of life. Both also to some extent accounted for the way her children's nature-study books all started at her back door, as she had gone on her walks with Fannie in childhood. Home was especially important to Trekkie. As well as speaking to her artistic integrity, even her exclusion from established artistic circles might perhaps be explained by her being an immigrant. On 7 June 1951 she wrote about her painting, "I must respond to the visual effects of the world around me – but I cannot quietly paint somewhat New English or London Group pictures." While moving forward, she kept thinking back to the warmth, the flowers, smells, and colours of her Natal childhood. "I must simplify tone. I have gone on refining too much. I must be positive in shape and colour and out of this arrive at atmosphere as much as is necessary. It makes drawing all the more important because it is from precision of draughtsmanship that solidity must come."

✿✿✿

At Easter 1949 she decided to keep a diary. On 8 May, sitting with Ian who was in London for surgery, she recorded that "27 years or so and 500 yards or so away from the Slade and Peter, I am now treated perfunctorily as Mrs. Ian Parsons and TR has melted off somewhere." By the time of her entry on 21 November 1950 she had decided that diary-writing was "like being an insect collector … only it is oneself one puts the pin through, one's own wings one spreads out in the little glass case."

She believed "the past to be part of the present and then the future." But she felt divided and pinned down, and being a woman, was looking for a way to live as a painter as well as a better way to paint. Hers was what she called the eternal female dilemma. She needed privacy and silence to work, and her concentration was interfered with by the need of relatives and her own guilt when she didn't rise to it. Leonard too drew on her time, but he also made a room for her in what had been Virginia's writing lodge. Trekkie called it her Blue Ark. Was she reminded of the name that Dora Carrington, Dorothy Brett, and Katherine Mansfield gave in 1916 to the house they shared on Gower Street? They thought of their "Ark" as floating them toward a better future. Was that Trekkie's intention too? She said that "work alone has a door heading outwards."

Her portraits were usually unadorned frontal views of friends and housekeepers. But her still lifes often looked through an open window to her garden and the Downs or through city curtains to a house across the street. Experimenting with "a penknife into the paint" on 7 June 1949, she was "covering all with simple clear colour, no radiated shadows and expressing the form with clear precise line and very slight lights and darks worked into the mass of colour." This style freed her "from the burden of gradated shadow without removing the beauty of solid form in space. Design can be kept clear and definite and colour much more personal and independent." Like all artists she needed the support of gallerists and critics in order to make her way in the art market and, although Leonard was helpful in discussing painting with her, she had no professional champion at the London galleries. When her pictures were exhibited they were not the sort people recognized across a crowded room, and after the war she was considered too old to be on the rise anyway.

On 19 June 1952 she took three paintings to the "Leicester" and was met by proprietor Ernest Brown, who "took me into the inner room, was very civil and quite friendly. Looked at them carefully. Liked the one of L best of which he said – 'This is very good' but also that it was unsalable and finally choose the greenish shouldered Anneliese and the one of Ian at Sanary. It was all absolutely painless. This time there was no suffocating emotional surge to deal with. I was calm and cool. How much I wish I could regularly get pictures shown without turmoil."

But in August she had a letter saying they had not hung either of her paintings. "I think I will not send any pictures to a show again. It is better just to accept the fact that I will never succeed and paint for myself." In the seventies and eighties she had six exhibits in Lewes at the Southover Gallery owned by Anthony and Deirdre Bland. Max Reinhardt told me that at one he attended in 1974 the exhibition sold out so quickly that Ian replenished it with pictures he took off the walls at Juggs until Trekkie realized what he was doing and stopped him. But even then, in the London art world Lewes was another country.

In November 1952, after finishing *England Under Four Queens*, which sold ten thousand copies, and sending off the colour plates for the second part of *Living Things*, she sat in her Blue Ark and began to read the extracts Leonard was pulling from Virginia's diaries for publication. They are "almost entirely about work. They are absorbing. I think about them on and off all day. Being here in this house of course increases their power over one." Trekkie would be the first of the millions of women who continue to look to Virginia's writing and life for inspiration:

> How hard she worked. And never let herself off. She notes the day as being her father's birthday, in one place – "he would be such and such an age had he lived" – Thank god, she says, he hadn't – "I would have been able to write no books." That is true. This thought has gone through me too … Too much of life has to be lived at an angle other than one's own … I do admire her. She was a worker, and single-minded. Nothing but her work mattered. It is interesting to see that she altered slightly all through at the change of life, not in her purpose but as in cooking you

> alter the whole flavour of a dish by throwing in – say – a pinch of cinnamon. So she had a slightly different quality. I imagine I perceive something of the same sort happening to me. But what is behind me compared to what she had done at 50? I have struggled as single mindedly – and from a lower swamp – both as regards position and endowments – only better health, I have that.

But just as she began to paint, relatives would arrive and Ian's publishing friends. And being fifty was "a dreary business make no mistake, recognizing age in oneself. I have reached that stage in my looks' decay when it seems absurd to repine. And I don't much. In my youth I did not dig the mine of my beauty very deeply, at least now I need not become desperate because it is becoming exhausted." But it bothered her "feeling there was not much time to go." On bad days she felt "like a punctured tyre."

Then there was Norah Smallwood. While Leonard and Ian respected the divide, Norah kept turning up unexpectedly. "She's like dry rot in a house," Trekkie wrote in May 1952. "She seeps into everything. It is only by removing myself altogether that I feel I have any privacy from her. I hate her and that's a fact and I despise myself for doing so." Not only was Norah Ian's mistress. She was seven years younger than Trekkie and by then Ian's publishing partner. At the press she terrified everyone with her sharp tongue. In responding to Trekkie's dust-jacket design for Lorens van der Post's *The Face Beside the Fire* (1953), Norah said it was "so nice – but change the colour and make this a little and that a little different. L agrees you should not fidget people who produce work for you with these little niggling alterations. You might say no it won't do, but if you niggle about, you change the character of a person's work."

Trekkie had a successful record as a jacket designer and a children's writer and illustrator, yet she was deeply stung by Norah's casual assault, the more so because she was an honest judge of her own work and had always destroyed what she thought didn't measure up. She retrenched into her painter self, rationalizing as she reworked the jacket that she did not mind. "I regard such jobs as dressmaking really and up to a point fit the customer as well as I can." But when a few months earlier she discovered that Ian had told Norah she'd been trying to wear contact lenses after she'd asked him to tell no one, she "roared off" and then wished "to god I had not such a violent passionate nature. How can I learn to control my idiotic fits of gloom. It is absurd I suppose to mind so much but I do." Loyalty. Ian's to their arrangement seemed less than hers. Yet she felt the guilt and shame.

Nearing sixty she lamented that she had "dithered from emptiness to emptiness. I have not exactly fallen between two stools. I have sat with half my behind on a different stool – painting and human relationships." She'd been navigating between painting and earning money with children's books and dust jackets at a time when women were supposed to just have children, which Ian had wanted and she had not, filling the gap for him with those of relatives and friends. I thought of what she'd told Dadie Rylands about Lili Briscoe. Was she wrong and Virginia Woolf right? And Trekkie was about to travel to Israel in 1957 and to Ceylon in 1960 with Leonard, both very important excursions for him. In her diary she wrote more wonderfully indiscreet accounts than he left of both trips and made a list of the flowers they found on their walks and his aches and pains, which she worried about. She painted no pictures. Was she fostering his career as she did Ian's at the expense of her own? She'd spent her days helping her men live and, even taking her quick-tempered outbursts into account, seemingly without effort, while in her dairy on 1 March 1958 she wrote, "more and more I am filled with the sense of failure – in every way, a failure to produce anything and failure in relationships."

I knew this conflict of desire, as the painter Celia Paul put it. I was privileged in many ways and had had more freedom to work than any married woman of my acquaintance. Yet I too had been stretched between loyalties to my husband and son, my students, and my desire to write whatever I was writing. In the three years between the day I first read the correspondence and the day I posted the proofs of *Love Letters* to Jenny Uglow, I'd had to fly to London every time I could clear a week from the classroom, and to work non-stop in archives and interviewing people when I was there. To get the grants that paid those expenses, I'd also prepared *Reflections* for publication and written Charlotte Haldane's entry for the *New Dictionary of National Biography*. So it was not surprising that one exhausting afternoon at Dawson I told my novelist office-mate Ray Smith that I empathized with Trekkie. "Stop identifying with her," he snapped back. "She's not fiction."

I had come across many commonalities: I too was a terrible speller; the Seurat poster in Trekkie's kitchen we also had in our bedroom in Richelieu Place; from her travels she'd kept a postcard of La Vierge de Moulins and there was a large poster of the centre panel of the triptych in our country house in Sutton; Sheila Dickinson lived in Rye where I so often stayed with the Rudés; like Trekkie I was accident-prone. The list was long, the last entry occasioned by a letter I found in a new Hogarth Press edition of *Flush* that an old student had sent me from the Cambridge sale of Ryland's books after he died. Trekkie had inscribed the novel to "Darling Dadie, with fondest love from Trekkie, 1983." In her introduction to the book she'd written something no critic I'd read had figured – that "in all her loving relationships" Virginia had "protected herself by half pretending to be an animal." Had Trekkie done the same with Leonard? Especially in their early correspondence he had called her animal names too. Pretty quickly she had snarled at the habit, but later when she felt vulnerable she had signed off as "Your – your what? Tiger it once was." The letter I found inside the book from her to Dadie was dated 29 August 1987. It described a lightning strike at Juggs that landed so close to her in the kitchen that she was nearly struck. A few days before *Flush* arrived there had been a storm in Sutton and blue lightning had shot a foot out of a wall socket close to our bed.

But no – I did not identify with Trekkie and, good friend that he was, Ray was presumptive in suggesting I might. Did he identify with the lovers of his fictional women in the lacy black underwear he dressed them in? Or with Vronsky in *Anna Karenina*, whose life he relived annually with his students? Perhaps he did. He preferred the tragic cut to the everyday fade when it came to women. "No," I repeated angrily. "I said empathize not identify." Yet for all its permutations, in her struggle to remain undividedly dedicated to her painting, Trekkie's life was similar to so many professional women's and I wanted readers to know that, to hear the tear in her voice. Did that mean I was losing my prized critical distance?

Shortly after Leonard died in August 1969 Ian took Trekkie to Tunisia. On 11 October she wrote in her diary, "I am half in Sussex all the time, wanting and dreading the return." The finishing of a book has the same desired release and the same fear of absence. You give yourself over to it completely and it changes you, and then you must let it go and live on without it, as it does without you. And writing biography has an additional price. In the beginning I had wanted to write Trekkie's biography. Instead I had turned her letters into her autobiography and had become the biographer of her own story. When I started *Love Letters* I'd put her photo on my desk and looked her straight in the eye every morning as I wrote the introduction and added notes and pieces from her diary. When the book was finished and I put her picture away I missed her. This was not sentimentality, or identification in the way Ray had suggested. For a while a biographer lives in her subject. It's the worst and the best thing about the work. When Sheila Dickinson rang to thank me for sending her the book she said, "you must be elated – and devastated at the loss."

Did *Love Letters* do Trekkie justice? I don't know. Writer Mary Ann Caws told me how much Carolyn Heilbrun, the distinguished feminist writer and academic, had appreciated the book, which she read just before she died. And the publisher Judy Taylor Hough, who couldn't read for a long time after her husband died, said *Love Letters* got her reading again, that it gave her such pleasure she read it straight through. But did it do Trekkie justice?

By not clipping the correspondence I had let her speak for herself. She was honest and well aware of how lives change in retrospect. And she understood the narrowness of opportunity within most lives. For all her angst and sometimes feisty anger I don't think she'd have altered the arrangement she, Leonard, and Ian lived. She wanted to paint better. What artist does not? That she kept trying is what impressed me, and the way she de-dramatized herself. "We live a while and then we die and living we make a great fuss and dying are as if we had not been," she wrote in her diary one winter's day as she prepared supper for Leonard in Monk's kitchen.

8

Max Reinhardt
Gentleman Publisher

I don't know who Max Reinhardt thought I was when he wrote in the late 1980s to ask if he could publish *Reflections*. His letter was acquiescent, and astonishing since Graham Greene had not yet agreed to my doing the book. Only later did I learn that Max's partners had recently sold The Bodley Head behind his back and that he and Graham were continuing to publish together under the Reinhardt Books imprimatur.

Elizabeth Bowes-Lyon, the Queen Mother's relative whom Max had hired as his assistant publisher in the new venture, used to ring me early in the morning with London gossip and messages from Max. A few days after I sent her my introduction to the book, she said Max wanted me to write myself into the essay. "Literary critics don't do that," I replied. "Well, Max wants you to so I'll wait." And she did as I began slowly to think out loud: "One day in the depths of the Canadian winter a letter arrived from Graham Greene ..." I can't remember how long that opening took. Not long, I think, once I got used to hearing my own voice. Of course Max was right, as he was about most publishing things.

Even though I'd written a couple of books and many articles, and had been reviewing for the *Toronto Star* for some time, until I met

Max I had thought of myself as an academic and not as a writer. Knowing him tipped the balance. As Euan Cameron, who was head of publicity at The Bodley Head for years said, you always felt flattered to be one of Max's guests. Whenever I was in London he took me to lunch at the Poissonnerie on Sloane Avenue. The fish was excellent and the conversation anecdotal in a publishing way, Max assuming that I knew the people he was talking about, as eventually I came to. Only slowly did his own story spill out. It was the most interesting.

For a Montrealer, everything seemed to happen very fast – the finishing of *The Dangerous Edge* and the putting together of *Reflections*, which was published in June 1990 and thereafter in many languages. Reinhardt Books was serviced by Penguin, and Elizabeth's office was in their building at 27 Wright's Lane. I first went there just after the Ayatollah Khomeini had issued his *fatwa* against Salman Rushdie. The building boasted a security system tighter than the Pentagon, the block around it closed off in a veritable fortress defensive. At the entrance a policeman with a machine gun apologized profusely for being armed as he frisked me.

"Good reviews, good reviews!" Max boomed theatrically about the reception of *Reflections*. Except from one fellow in the *Financial Times* who didn't like Graham's politics and another in the *Irish Times* who didn't like his brand of Catholicism, they were excellent reviews and by December the book was on many best-for-Christmas lists. By then Graham was dying and Max was not well but they were both pleased. So was I. I'd never had publicity like that before. I stood mesmerized in front of Hatchards's window. Max had insisted on the importance of having "Selected and Introduced by ..." on the cover. When Louise Dennys took my name off the front of her redesigned Canadian jacket for marketing purposes, he was more furious than I was. But in London, for one morning, I smiled at the Reinhardt/Viking/Penguin jacket in bookshop windows and watched people inside pick up and buy the book.

So Max and I became friends and until his death in 2002 I saw him whenever I was in London, through the writing of Charlotte's biography and *Love Letters*. That book interested him especially because, after the merger of Chatto, The Bodley Head, and Jonathan Cape in 1973, Ian Parsons had been his partner and he knew many of the people Trekkie and Leonard wrote about to one another. Elizabeth sometimes came with us to the Poissonnerie; sometimes we went alone. Then, in July 1992 Max needed open heart surgery for the second time and thereafter his wife, Joan, gave us smoked salmon sandwiches on thinly sliced brown bread and a glass of wine in his study and left us to talk. He was frail and by then eager to tell me what had happened at The Bodley Head.

For some years I'd encouraged him to write his memoirs. After the surgery I suggested he talk into a tape recorder. Belinda McGill, who had been his secretary for decades at The Bodley Head and was very fond of him, had begun to work for him again and, when one day he agreed that I turn on the recorder I'd brought, she transcribed our conversation. Taping our talks became a project we devised to interest Max, whose mind was never as sharp after the long hours he was on the heart lung machine for the second time.

At some point he asked if I would write his memoirs for him. He didn't tell me what he had in mind. I thought a full-blown autobiography and said I wasn't a ghostwriter. "Of course not," he answered. "Your name will be on the cover." And we left it at that until the book was almost finished. When I saw that it was turning into a small Christmas book for his friends like the ones he had often published with a story or a new book introduction of Graham's, I suggested he call it *Memories* rather than *Memoirs*. The book would remember only happy times, he said. The other stories were for me to tell when he was dead. Those were about the takeover of The Bodley Head. Max, I came to realize, hated unpleasantness. Avoiding it was part of his charm, and perhaps his downfall.

Once I'd agreed to help him he asked how much I wanted for doing the work. I later learned that he used to ask his Bodley Head employees when they were hired how much they could manage on. I had no idea what my time was worth. Alan said to ask Vincent. Vincent said,

"Ask him for £5000 but he won't pay you that." Ever embarrassed to talk about money, I left the pound sign off the 5000 when I wrote back, hoping Max would think it a typo. But he understood perfectly well what I'd done and rang me in Montreal. "You didn't say Canadian or American dollars, or British pounds," he laughed. "Well, Max," I answered, "given the choice, I'd be a fool not to say pounds." And so it was fixed. Did I want the money in cash or a cheque? A cheque would be fine.

I took a teaching term off and we rented a small flat in Queen Court for the winter, arriving in London on a Friday morning in January 1998, a few weeks after the Montreal ice storm had left us at below-zero temperatures without heat or electricity in Richelieu Place for five days. London was unusually warm and I went out with Max's cheque in hand to open a bank account, since we'd closed our British one a few years before. At three banks close to Russell Square I was told the same thing – because of money laundering I now needed proof of British residency to open an account. I had one manager telephone our Montreal bank and, when that didn't help, rang Coutts Bank myself, the bank on which Max's cheque was written. Oh yes, Coutts knew Mr Reinhardt. But they too were very sorry. They could not cash the cheque.

By mid-afternoon I realized I had to phone Max. He laughed and said that was why he'd asked if I wanted the money in cash and to send Alan over. Joan would go to the bank. Empty briefcase in hand, Alan took a taxi as he promised me he would. Joan said she was terrified carrying the money in her purse from their bank around the corner from Onslow Square. Alan stuck the £5000 in his briefcase, had a drink with Max and took the Tube back to Bloomsbury. Getting across town by taxi had taken too long, he said, as he made himself another martini. By Monday our old Hampstead friend, Rufus Gilday, had put what we didn't need of the cash in his account for safekeeping and we'd settled into our usual library routine with long lunches at Vincent's table, and me spending an afternoon a week with Max.

In the end there was only one glitch with the work itself. Max was paying the bill and since I left London in the summer and didn't get back until October, I suppose Joan came to think she had final control of *Memories*. I first saw this when several little things were changed in my edited copy. Not surprisingly, the taped conversations swirled about. As I saw it, my job was to write Max's stories chronologically and in his voice, which was not easy to catch, and I was concerned that it not be fiddled with. Joan's concern was that events appear as she wanted them to. Belinda's was to replace my text hoping Joan wouldn't notice. But just before I returned in October she rang to say that Joan had added her name to the cover.

When I got there Max was a little embarrassed. "Now this is what we'll do," he said. His name was to be up front, and mine below his as "having been told to." Joan, who was in the dining room across the hall from Max's study at the time, was to be called editor on this cluttered cover. I had already decided I didn't want to be named on Max's book which, if charming, had become curiously uninformative. So without a pause I said, "I know what we agreed but this is your book, Max, and I don't think anyone's name should be on the cover but yours." Belinda jumped up immediately and rushed out to tell Joan what a great idea it was that only Max's name be on the jacket. He was happy the problem had been so easily solved. Joan was graciously furious but there wasn't much she could do. So it was settled. Paper and typeface were carefully chosen by Joan, and *Memories* was handsomely published privately for friends at Christmas 1998 with nothing in it about what had happened to The Bodley Head. I had Belinda's transcripts of our conversations. Max gave me the top copy and thanked me inside for my help. And except for that one day there had been nothing but pleasure in playing his ghost.

I continued to see Joan and Max whenever I was in London. When he died Belinda rang and sent me an invitation to the celebration of his life at the Garrick Club. Pieces of *Memories* had been read at the crematorium she said, and bits from Wally Lambert's *The History of*

The Bodley Head. At the Garrick Judy Taylor talked about her publishing years with Max, and when I asked if she would write his biography she said no, you do it and introduced me to her old colleagues. Judy had made the children's division of the press more profitable than Max's enviable fiction list for many years, and from 1967 had been a director of the firm, then its deputy manager. Richard Attenborough talked about what Max had done for the Royal Academy of Dramatic Art. Broadcaster Michael Charlton read publisher Ian Chapman's message as Chapman had been taken ill. Euan Cameron stood on a chair to read Lord Jack Ashley's eulogy. Joan recalled fond memories of forty-six years of marriage and ended with Max's favourite recommendation, "Let's have a drink." So we drank magnums of champagne and remembered Max when he had run the best imprint in English.

When I began to write Max's biography I didn't realize I was writing about the transition of British publishing from the independent imprints, which like The Bodley Head were often personally owned, to the conglomerates. I knew what had happened to Max but I couldn't then make sense of the benefits and drawbacks of mergers and acquisitions, or read complicated financial reports. Probably if I had known where I was going I'd never have begun the journey. But I'd come off the success of *Love Letters,* and after helping Max with *Memories* I thought it logical that I do the biography. No one else seemed to want to and Joan agreed that I should. So I began interviewing The Bodley Head people and spending as much time as I could with Judy Taylor.

To begin I needed a quick lesson in the mechanics of publishing, and Sue Bradley's taped interviews with Judy, Belinda, and Max for *Book Trade Lives* were housed in the British Library's Sound Archive. There I discovered that books used to be packed in corrugated cardboard and the sides flattened with wooden blocks before each bundle was wrapped in brown paper for delivery and tied with a slip knot.

Judy Taylor talked about being the only woman, and the only children's editor, on the Publishers Association Council in the early 1970s. In 1971 she was awarded the MBE for her contribution to British publishing. Even thirty years later the surprise at having broken into a man's world was still in her voice. There were quirky details in her interview that allowed me to reconstruct scenes. When she came out of the Bodley Head office in Bow Street she'd find vegetables left for her under her car by the Covent Garden market people whose stalls were nearby. They also saved her a parking space in the morning.

Belinda's description of the rush in the summer of 1968 to polish the translation of Solzhenitsyn's *Cancer Ward* held funny anecdotes, like that of ringing her doctor husband late one day to ask where you dispose of an amputated leg and typing "in a bin" into the text as he replied. Then there was the story of her first week at The Bodley Head in 1964. Max's closest friend, Ralph Richardson, who was also on his board of directors, had come for lunch. Max handed Belinda some smoked salmon and a loaf of brown bread and asked her to make them sandwiches, which she did. He then brought her a bottle of chilled wine and a new-fangled corkscrew, the now ubiquitous kind with arms that you push down to raise the cork. When she couldn't figure out how it worked Ralph piped in, "Maxie darling, next time you interview a secretary don't bother about the shorthand and typing speeds. Just give her a bottle opener, and if she can't do it, don't employ her." Listening to these tapes was like being at The Bodley Head. I could not have recreated place and time without them.

Sue's tapes with Max were different. Between the many afternoons I'd spent with him and when she interviewed him, his memory seemed to have grown more imprecise than I remembered. Or had it? The stories he told were the same as those he'd told me. They were told more slowly and some of the detail had faded but as Sue waited more patiently than I probably did for his answers, every so often Max added something unexpected.

Oral history is the devil to work with. Tempted as I was to use Sue's interview transcripts as I would a good index to a book, it was when I kept my finger off the fast-forward button that I found what I needed. It came in pauses between words, in the intonation of Max's voice as he formed an answer to a question I already knew the answer to, in a hesitation, or a laugh. I suspect he was as surprised as I was by the little revelations that tumbled out while Sue waited, for Max was the consummate gentleman not used to revealing things, especially about himself. In a pause the direction of his sentence could change and as he re-formed it something astonishing was sometimes revealed. I'd stop, go back and listen to it again, then stop again.

After Max died Belinda found thousands of his papers in the Onslow Square basement. So back we went to London, this time to a flat in Whitfield Street from which Alan could walk to the library to finish his research for *Mr. Charlotte Brontë*, his biography of Arthur Bell Nicholls, and I could get across town quickly once a week to meet Belinda, who'd help me fill a taxi with as many large plastic bins of paper as I could read in seven days. The only exercise I got that dark winter was in the late afternoons when, after hours of taking notes, I'd fill my shopping cart with Max's letters and business papers and wheel it to a copy shop a mile away, stopping for groceries at Sainsbury's on Tottenham Court Road on the way back.

When I reread some of the letters recently in the British Library where they are now housed to find something for a friend, I came across a spelling error in one of mine to Max. The head of manuscripts laughed when I told him that I'd instinctively picked up my pencil to correct the mistake and as quickly pulled back my hand before it touched the paper. The keepers, he said, had caught someone adding to a folder to make himself look more important. I didn't tell him how I'd carted the papers home from the copy shop that winter under my grocery bags.

❂ ❂ ❂

The bins of paper from Max's house contained the facts and fragments of his publishing life, and as I took notes and photocopied what I knew I would need when I got back to Montreal his biography began to take shape. He had huge skill in dealing with temperamental authors. Who would have thought that after Georgette Heyer moved with Graham from Heinemann to The Bodley Head in 1963 she would bombard Max until her death with long letters deprecating her publisher, her own books, the tax man, her typists, the workmen who came to renovate her house – her shot had wide scatter. Max was a little frightened of her at first. "I'm not formidable, am I, Max?" she had boomed at him across the table at Rules one early day. "I don't frighten you, do I?" He gained confidence when he met her husband, Ronald Rougier, and their son Sir Richard, who put him up for election at the Garrick, and with whom he played bridge. Max, he said, was among the top four players at the Club, and Georgette Heyer greatly appreciated his skill after her dinner parties.

Once Max got to know her, he decided she was charming, affectionate, and loyal. He appreciated her professionalism. Her readership in Australia was huge, and the letters showed that she never missed the date Max needed a typescript in order to have a new book printed, bound, and delivered for shipping there in time for the Christmas sales. She was one of Max's best-selling authors but critics sometimes said her work was not in the top bracket. If his defence of her showed his lack of literary sophistication, it also proved his personal loyalty to his authors. He told one critic Heyer knew her military history so well that when an elderly gentleman wrote to ask what part his great-grandfather's regiment had played at the Battle of Waterloo, she instantly recognized the regiment. If true, why hadn't she answered the letter? Because, Max replied, the regiment was the only one to have fled the field and she didn't have the courage to tell the old fellow. Then thinking he might have made Heyer look too soft he added that he'd recently been on a West Indian beach where he sat beside a Canadian mining tycoon who carried half a dozen of her books in his beach bag and told Max of the enormous pleasure she'd given all his mining colleagues over the years.

Among the papers were scenes from Max's seven-year courtship of Charlie Chaplin, along with Graham's letter about the first cuts he'd made to Chaplin's autobiography, the cuts he'd told me about decades before when he was testing my loyalty of silence. "I treated what I read quite cavalierly," Graham had written, then asked how best he and Max should tell Chaplin what he'd done. There were details of their many visits to Vevey. Especially interesting were those from the evening Chaplin had read them what he'd written about the poverty of his childhood, his half-brother Sydney and his mother, crying all the while. Next morning Graham had told him the autobiography was going to be wonderful, that he didn't believe in many things but he did believe in good writing, writing that conveyed the right kind of emotion, and what Charlie had read to them was first rate.

But Chaplin was not easy to work with. A telegram from Max's typist begged him to get her out. "I hope I do not have a breakdown," she wrote. "Please come to my rescue and arrive as soon as possible and stay as long as possible." And there was a letter to Max from James Michie, his then newly hired editorial director, who had been sent to Vevey and wrote back to say Chaplin was "impossible, a monster of egotism." When Graham encouraged Chaplin by telling him he'd read "the proofs of the first part of your autobiography with enormous pleasure," he sent Max a private addendum asking how many more words they would need to cut.

I found the Chaplins' 1964 Christmas card in the bins. It had a photo of Charlie and Oona on a sofa surrounded by their many children, each reading *My Autobiography* in a different language. The book had just been published and had already sold over half a million copies, recouping Max's bold half-a-million-dollar advance to Chaplin for it. In November 1961 Max had had to borrow the money from his own bank because Chaplin had still not signed the contract. When Max insisted he needed a signature in order to finance the advance, Chaplin had written back: "For your business convenience, this is to confirm our verbal agreement whereby you will have world publishing book rights of my autobiography on the conditions we have discussed, subject to contract."

Among the papers there were many letters from Ralph Richardson, who was always lonely on tour and would write tenderly to Max about their weekly squash games, and ask him to send books and gossip about The Bodley Head. Along with copies of the newspaper clippings and tributes to Ralph when he died in October 1983, Max had kept a letter of his own written ten years earlier to The Bodley Head's Australian agent. "When you meet him you will be enchanted by him. I want you to know that he is my oldest and my best friend. When he was last in Australia he went into book shops and said modestly, 'My name is Richardson. I'm a publisher. Have you got any of our books here?' I'm sure he will want to do the same again."

From the papers it was clear that in his best years, Max was an enabler. He demanded loyalty and returned it. He honoured people with small tributes, with directorships, some with larger favours. He was free of pomposity, conducting business on a handshake as with Chaplin or, as with Graham Gordon at Butterworths in September 1984 to whom he sold H. Foulkes Limited, his original publishing company, with a tap on the shoulder at a book trade function and the words "Ready when you are." But Max was no egalitarian. He had a deep-rooted egotism which gave him his authority. While his even temper, graciousness, and desire for fun helped him attract and keep the best people in every part of the publishing process, he was a businessman who liked the company of authors and the feel of books more than he liked to read them. He helped his staff get on with making the books they wanted to while he continued to pay them in the bottom third of publishers and to live lavishly himself.

❂❂❂

The letters provided me weeks of fun and the first part of Max's publishing story – his chance meeting with Ralph Richardson on a squash court at Kensington Close soon after he arrived in London in January 1939, through the setting up of Max Reinhardt Ltd to publish George Bernard Shaw and Ellen Terry's letters in 1949, the purchase of The

Bodley Head from Sir Stanley Unwin in 1956, the arrival of Graham as constant adviser in 1957, the success of Chaplin's autobiography in 1964, and the other coups that followed in the first decades of Max's Bodley Head. Jill Black, who edited many of Graham's books, called them the champagne years.

But as the pile of financial papers about what had happened thereafter got larger I began to understand why none of the people I'd met at Max's Garrick Club celebration had wanted to write his biography. And the deeper I investigated the circumstances of the company's demise the more I worried that if I wrote what Max had not wanted included in his Christmas book someone might sue me. So as spring arrived I pulled my grocery cart to the copy shop twice a day and mailed bundles of duplicated business papers to Montreal, putting off what I knew would be a long slog. And I rang Eric de Bellaigue, who had written knowledgeably about the postwar mergers and acquisitions in British publishing.

He had shown that from the late 1960s, British communication groups and publishing companies had begun to combine their resources. Then American companies, predominantly with media interests, had quickly come into the British business, and soon afterward there had been a reversal of capital investment. Successful publishing requires good books and good marketing. The Bodley Head had always produced a quality product and, as currency controls eased and the markets deregulated in the mid-seventies, Max needed a larger and more sophisticated distribution and sales force. The Americans had these complex organizational skills. But Max wanted to keep his firm entirely British. So in 1973 he joined Chatto and Jonathan Cape, who had come together in 1969 in need of the same services.

Through the recession of 1980 with its near lethal combination of domestic inflation and surging sterling, that merger seemed successful. When Carmen Callil took Virago into the service arrangement in 1982 she firmly believed that the distribution and warehousing of her books would improve under the new umbrella. She pretty quickly discovered that it cost her more to publish a book though the joint service company than when Virago was alone.

Max's business papers confirmed Eric's analysis of what had happened. But several of his personal letters showed that he had begun to worry about the joint company's finances shortly after The Bodley Head merger with Chatto and Jonathan Cape, which was some years earlier than Eric suggested. Certainly by the time Virago became a partner, Max was saying openly that the service company was being irresponsibly run. Whatever the individual firms made was put into a joint kitty and everyone took out of it what was needed to pay advances for future lists. The problem was that no one knew until months later when the bank statements arrived what the individual company's overheads were. The result was that between 1982 and 1984 the selling and distribution costs fell a percentage point but the administrative and editorial costs rose about 5 per cent, raising the total operating costs of CVBC as a percentage of turnover from 36.6 per cent to 40.2 before anyone realized what was happening – except Max.

His personal letters revealed his increasing anxiety as the Net Book Agreement, whereby publishers had set the price of books since 1900, wound down and library and hard cover purchases, which had been the bread and butter of quality publishing for years, fell off steadily. Max complained that the joint system wasn't good enough to meet the new demand for paperbacks, which the reading public not surprisingly preferred at a third the price of hardbacks. Then there were agents who, at about the same time, were changing the author-publisher relationship that was so important to him and epitomized The Bodley Head style. His partners were happy to work with them. Max hated them and believed that authors who used them paid more tax unnecessarily on their earnings than if he paid them, as he did Graham and sometimes Georgette Heyer, in agreed sums at regular intervals rather than in lump advances. But many authors disagreed. Agents were bidding up larger profits for them and encouraging them to move from publisher to publisher to get them.

❂❂❂

At the beginning of 1981 Judy Taylor left after thirty years. She continued to come to the office one day a month and to work on the children's books from Gloucestershire where she moved with her new husband, Richard Hough. But she gave up her place on all Max's boards, The Bodley Head, the holding company with Cape and Chatto that Virago would soon join, and the Canadian and Australian companies. She had been Max's right hand and he'd expected her to take over the firm when he retired. After the 1973 merger she said the three houses began to lose their individuality and she didn't want to stay. At first it was little things that bothered her. The books were now warehoused at Grantham and if she wanted a copy to give someone she couldn't just go and get it as she used to because The Bodley Head's trade counter had been closed. The larger changes mattered more. Like Max, she knew that budgets, turnover, expected subsidiary benefits, cash flow, and so on were better managed in house by their own staff than by people who were far removed from the scene of operation.

Max was shocked by her departure, and he was increasingly out of his depth in the new system. To replace her he hired David Machin, who had worked for Cape and the Society of Authors before he came to The Bodley Head. David was comfortable with agents. So was Tom Maschler, who managed Cape with Graham C. Greene. Max never got along with Maschler, but he trusted Graham C. because he was Graham Greene's nephew, even though the author had warned him not to. And, being always with people he called "distinguished," Max misjudged his own social position in the English hierarchy, which made him even more vulnerable to the younger Greene, who told me he thought Max a rogue.

In February 1984 when Greene and Maschler asked Max to sell them half his shares, he did. He was sixty-nine. Joan didn't want to take over from him, and he figured their daughters were unlikely to be interested in publishing in the future. Max was, by his own admission, getting tired. Ralph Richardson had died only a few months earlier and Max was himself plagued by intermittent back pain from his squash and tennis accidents. He thought Graham C. would take care of things and believed that with 25 per cent of the holding company he could still block anything he disagreed with because Greene and Maschler had only 21.2 percent each. But as they joined forces against him Max soon realized his error.

Keeping each imprint at a separate address was expensive and Greene suggested they could economize by taking a twenty-five-year lease on 32 Bedford Square, the premises adjoining the Cape building at number 30. That building would be refurbished for Cape – it turned out at exorbitant expense – and The Bodley Head could move into number 30. Max didn't like the idea but his lease in Bow Street was up and the Covent Garden Opera House had its eye on the whole block, so he agreed. The same year he sold his accountancy text book company, HFL, to Butterworths, keeping the name as a trading company for future use. HFL had long been nicknamed High Finance Limited by Max's staff because it had helped carry them financially from the start.

The Bodley Head people were never happy in Bedford Square. In early September 1985 Max had a massive heart attack after a board meeting at the top of number 32 where a change in the firm's paperback arrangements was announced, a change that many of his staff volubly disagreed with. He had to have a valve replaced during open-heart surgery and from then on worked mostly at home. As the service group's debt continued to rise, Max became convinced they would need a large company to take a stake in the firm or to buy them out, and he began to talk to his friends at Penguin. He must have anticipated this when he sold HFL. He now sold his Australian building and some Bodley Head copyrights, six of Agatha Christie's novels among them.

Soon his staff were forced to share copyediting, production, design, publicity, and rights services with Cape to save money. The firms were supposed to remain separate but there were redundancies. Then Maschler and Greene floated a rights issue and resented Max for refusing to add more capital to the firm. Instead he continued to negotiate a different arrangement for The Bodley Head and promised

Carmen Callil that he would support Virago's departure from the holding company. Meanwhile, Greene and Maschler were making other plans that ended in the sale of the group, including The Bodley Head, to Random House without Max's permission.

By January 1987 Graham C. was openly hostile to Max. He sent him a letter saying that the Max Reinhardt Ltd imprint, under which Max had sometimes sold books The Bodley Head hadn't wanted to publish, could now only be used with permission from the joint company. Max was furious. On 6 February he answered that he wanted The Bodley Head disentangled from the group, however difficult it might be to do. And he added a post-script: "Graham, with whom I had dinner last night, has been aware of the situation for some time and told me that he would not entrust his new novel, which is nearly ready, to The Bodley Head if he felt that its financial problems had not been solved." The feuding went public when the younger Greene retaliated by telling the *Times*'s "Londoner's Diary" that any rumours about Virago leaving the group were "pure fantasy."

Max and Graham planned their Bodley Head strategy over a bottle of claret and the English sausages Joan cooked for them, Graham's fried, Max's roasted. On 28 March, Graham responded publicly to his nephew's story: "Saying rumours of changes are pure fantasy seems to indicate that he is living himself in a fantasy world. Publishers depend on authors and I am sure that I am not the only author who will consider leaving the group should there be none of the necessary changes in the administration." Two days later Max disclosed in *The Independent* that he wanted to buy back The Bodley Head and run it privately again, not by committee.

Once I added these bare bones to what Max had told me and the plethora of newspaper clippings about the sale that I found among his papers, it was easy to fill in the details. But the story was factually complex to document and I'd never forgotten the power of William Shawn at *The New Yorker* when he covered up Penelope Gilliatt's plagiarism. I made sure my publisher had a solicitor check my typescript for libel, and I reworked a few paragraphs at his suggestion by being a little gracious to Greene and Maschler without diluting how they had disposed of The Bodley Head without Max's consent.

○ ○ ○

Max wanted to call his new imprint Max Reinhardt Books but the way The Bodley Head had been sold made that legally impossible. It didn't prevent him from surrounding himself with old friends. He would be chairman and managing director of Reinhardt Books and would make the editorial decisions with the help of Joan, who was named co-editor. Judy Taylor returned as his consulting editor. Headquarters were at Pelham Crescent. Everyone came and went to check in with him, and lunches with authors were taken in nearby restaurants. Penguin provided an office, along with distribution, sales, marketing, production and some editorial services, sharing the costs and profits of Max's books.

Max had always thrived on what he controlled and had an instinct to leave what he couldn't. In his youth he'd gone to Paris when Istanbul became hostile to foreigners, and as a young man he'd left Paris in the face of war, leaving his family for a kind of British life he'd learned in Istanbul from his gentle headmaster at the English High School for Boys. He'd been lucky. His Uncle Richard had financed his move. In London Harold Laski, who was chairman of the British Labour Party from 1926 to 1950 and had taught Max at the London School of Economics during the war, had guided him into British life. Ralph Richardson had taught him the role of British gentleman; Graham Greene had helped make him a British publishing giant. He seemed to have needed the approval of these men and, through the breakup of the holding company and the setting up of Reinhardt Books, Graham guided him again.

The manuscript of *The Captain and the Enemy* was delivered in mid-December 1987 and Graham soon brought in Christopher Hawtree's *Yours Etc.* (1989) and my *Reflections* (1990). He got Max to publish Vincent McDonnell's *The Broken Commandment* (1988), which won the Irish Guinness Peat Aviation First Fiction Award. It put Max and Graham prominently in the news as continuing to do what they had always done. Without the huge advances and publicity budgets of the conglomerates, they gave a chance to a new writer. Judy Taylor secured children's books, among them Maurice Sendak's *Caldecott & Co.* (1989). Joan's part was more domestic. Max was getting short of breath again and in need of an elevator. She moved them around the corner from Pelham Crescent into Onslow Square and, as his heart condition worsened, joined his authors' lunches and quietly removed that extra glass of wine from his reach as she ordered him fish without sauce, and no dessert.

When Graham died on 3 April 1991 Max lost more than an old friend. He made jokes with Roger Straus and Alastair Cook about getting old but his letters exposed his diminishing abilities. He was a clubable man who had operated on friendship, trust, and charm and he was now alone in the harsh world of conglomerate publishing. In July 1992 he needed open-heart surgery again and, although he carried on after it, neither he nor Reinhardt Books were the same.

In the end it was Belinda who helped him most, and perhaps the taping of his stories toward *Memories* and Sue Bradley's *Book Trade Lives*. Max's daughter, Veronica, said he was such a private man that only when she listened to the tapes did she begin to understand her father's past. She had never heard the disturbing story he told Euan Cameron about the impaled heads he had seen as a child on the Galata Bridge, or what it was like to be a Jew in Paris in 1938, or what had happened to his relatives other than his mother and Uncle Richard during the war. He had left all that for me to pull together. "He never told us anything," she said. "He just wanted everyone to be happy."

He had wanted the same thing at The Bodley Head and by reassuring his talented team about production money he had created conditions for several decades in which they produced some of the finest books in the world and built a children's list second to none. But while he was for the most part a gentle patriarch with the appearance of an immensely confident man, Belinda thought that being cut off from his family so early by war had left him more vulnerable than he looked. Many of his friends were older men who trusted him as a father would a son, so Belinda was probably right. He was proud to make them happy and he appreciated the praise and friendship they returned.

Even though Max knew that what happened at The Bodley Head was caused in the first instance by changes in publishing that were beyond his control, he continued to believe that if his partners had done what he'd advised, the group could have been saved and, if when its sale became inevitable they had allowed him to buy his firm back, he could have kept it going. In his failure on both counts I know he felt he had badly let his staff down. Perhaps that's why he so resented what his partners did to him. They diminished his sense of his own genteel responsibility. And perhaps in the end he discovered that he wasn't as good a business man as he thought.

What he never lost was his sense of humour. Shortly before he died Belinda took him in his wheelchair into the garden of the nursing home he was confined to. "What's wrong with me?" he asked her. "Why can't I go home?" When she carefully answered, "Well, Max, let's just say you've got a very serious case of old age," he laughed so hard she thought he'd topple his chair.

9

Pentimento

When I arrived back from a research week in London in May 2005, Alan told me he was due the next day to have laser treatment on his left eye. The right one had been hit by a squash ball twenty years earlier and although the damage had healed, in the last couple of years he'd lost its central vision. Now he'd developed macular degeneration in his good eye, which the alleged top retinal man in Montreal said he could stop with a laser. The result was blindness in fifty-five seconds. The doctor wouldn't admit an accident. But it was, and the result was permanent. Alan could no longer read. "You go on with your life," he said. "I can take care of myself." Of course it didn't quite work out that way. In the next ten years he never complained but he was sometimes overcome by the scale of his affliction, and so was I.

"Now this is what I can do," archaeologist and anthropologist Bruce Trigger insisted as soon as he heard what had happened. From then until his own death a year and a half later he read to Alan for two hours every Tuesday afternoon. Even after Bruce's penultimate stay in the Montreal General Hospital, where Governor General Michaëlle Jean came to his bedside to award him the Order of Canada, Bruce turned up to read. He was writing his autobiography that year, and I often heard these two old friends laughing behind our closed living room door as they shared stories about various Canadian figures in Bruce's past.

After a dinner party one evening when Alan was noticeably failing, writer Dorothy Eber praised him for never saying anything wrong, by which she meant anything out of context. If you can't see when someone's finished talking and someone else is about to start it's difficult to be part of robust conversation. As the years passed he got tired of following and where he had been central in Montreal's lively, hard-hitting dinner conversations he became increasingly silent. Other friends read to him too – historian Pierre Boulle, with whom he had golfed for years, and medievalist Richard Lock, with whom he shared an intimate knowledge of Shakespeare and a fondness for the Sherlock Holmes stories. On the phone from Toronto, Nicholas read Roy Jenkins's *Gladstone* to him among other books. And most days over breakfast I read, the last book being Michael Zantovsky's *Havel*, my Czech pronunciation being constantly corrected. He took to audio books fairly well. But Alan was a man used to reading and discussing so much that hadn't been recorded, and whose legally blind sight couldn't accommodate the computer aids then available, none of which were designed for intellectuals in any case.

Between us we got *Mr. Charlotte Brontë* finished and published to good reviews. And I completed Max's biography largely with the help of Nicholas, who came from Toronto when he could to stay with his father so I could fly to London for a week here and there. We had Sutton, where Alan knew the lie of the land so well that he was able to get about on his own for some time. And we had each other. In those ten years there were many pleasures and huge difficulties. Alan was enormously brave. He was also severely damaged. In the end I don't think he knew whose hand was doing things for him, his or mine. Like a biographer and her subject, we had become indivisible.

❂❂❂

There was no vaccine when I was four and had measles. Our Rosemount flat was quarantined. A uniformed officer from the City of Montreal's health department nailed a warning to our door and tied a ribbon across our corner of the second-floor landing outside it. Another medical directive was tied to the bottom of the communal staircase under which a few months earlier I had thrown the letter expelling me from kindergarten for sneaking out of class. I was kept in the dark to protect my eyes. Yellowish curtains blew in and out at the open window. It was supposed to be kept closed but my sensible British mother said I needed fresh air. When the health inspector rang the bell she would lower the window and tell me to say nothing. I recovered without the possible blindness or deafness he predicted. So did my little brother.

There was no vaccine for polio in my Rosemount years and there were outbreaks of it every summer. We were made to peel the skin off fruit to protect ourselves, especially off peaches, whose furry outsides my mother said might harbour the virus, and to wash our hands. We were not allowed to have popsicles in case the water in them was contaminated. Ice cream was different for some reason, but ice cream was only afforded on special occasions.

In my second summer as a student nurse I was posted to the Alexandra, the contagious diseases hospital in Pointe-Saint-Charles on the southern lip of Montreal. It was an old red brick building with a garden at the back where we used to take afternoon tea with our teachers and sometimes ate unskinned peaches. By then most children had been inoculated with the Salk vaccine, but few adults had. There were polio patients in iron lungs at the Alex, and people with TB waiting to be moved to a sanitorium. If the incoming sick were not too sick we students donned the official long and no doubt infested navy blue woollen cape with the hospital crest embroidered on the collar and rode the ambulances to pick them up.

Neil Compton had been recently discharged when I arrived. He must have caught polio in the late fifties because the head nurse, who seemed very old as most women over forty then did to the young, told us he'd been in an iron lung for a year. We were astonished when our rather straight-laced teacher said his wife had been right to end their marriage if she hadn't been able to stay the course. Still frog-breathing four years later, Neil taught me seventeenth-century literature from his wheelchair at Sir George Williams College, his face reddening deeply as his brilliant lectures spurted on. A senior Honours English student whom we fondly tagged "Neil's legs" helped him get about. Fairly soon he married again.

The following summer there was no vaccine when a meningitis epidemic broke out in Montreal. During my three-month pediatric stint at the Children's Hospital on Tupper Street I worked on the contagious ward for thirty-one consecutive nights in a surgical mask, gown, and gloves over my heavily starched Royal Victoria uniform. I washed my hands so often that halfway through August both had serious raw patches in the skin. The head nurse told me to cover the rawness with antibiotic ointment before I gloved, then to double-glove and keep the inside pair on for the full eight-hour shift, scrubbing the inner gloves as though they were my bare hands before I double-gloved again between patients. Two decades later our pathologist friend John Richardson told me that when he did autopsies at the Montreal General Hospital during the AIDS epidemic he double- and sometimes triple-gloved.

One of my classmates caught meningitis. We packed her comatosed body in ice and blew fans across her to lower her temperature, as we did for the children. She survived. One baby did not. A couple were left with cognitive damage. By the end of August my ears roared like a cataract and I was dizzy. I thought I was going mad. But it was only a middle-ear infection that nearly ruptured both drums. I was given antibiotics and sent back to the ward for an additional week, until the epidemic broke.

At the end of that meningitis summer I borrowed my mother's car to drive to the Laurentians with some friends and got stopped in traffic on St Lawrence Boulevard. In front of the bus to my left lay a beautiful young boy, his skull split clean. His dislodged brain glistened in the noon sun. His eyes were open, his lips closed, his legs still astride his fallen bike. The string-tied package he must have carried from the butcher shop behind the paralysed sidewalk crowd was just beyond his outstretched hand. With arms crossed over his bloodied apron the butcher watched from his carcass-hung window. This is the way that summer ended, with a bang not a whimper.

From 1974 until 1988, when John Stirling, our next door neighbour in Richelieu Place, died a few months short of a hundred, Alan and I had a drink with him every Tuesday at five-thirty. John was the eighth chancellor of Queen's University and the retired head of Cape Construction Company. He had grown up in Dundas, Ontario, the younger son of a country doctor who'd sent him off to Queen's at sixteen. John wanted to be an engineer. His father said fine, but first you have to study Arts. What you learn there will sustain you through life. So at twenty-three he had a BA and a BSc. By 1914 he was in charge of building the water and sewer systems in Canada's burgeoning towns. His elder brother went to war and was killed. John enlisted a year later in the Engineering Corps and was sent to France. He caught Spanish flu at war's end and, while somewhere up to 100 million people died from it, he lived.

Even when asked, he rarely talked about the war. Or about how he survived the pandemic. For him those stories had limited purchase. But he often told of the day he returned to Kingston. People strung bunting and flags across the street and dressed in their best to welcome their soldiers back. As John passed the laundry near the university, its owner rushed out to shake his hand and present him with the shirts he had left to be laundered three years earlier, all freshly starched.

❂❂❂

We count on the future. We plan for its rhythms and predictability even when COVID-19 sliced time into before and after like the First World War did John Stirling's life and Alan's blindness did ours. I watched how friends tried to regain control at the beginning of our pandemic years. One made order by walking for hours each day. Another baked bread and made jams. Several cleaned house endlessly with disinfectant. At eighty-one, my Dawson colleague Helen Wehden, who was already ill, could find no reason to go on and decided to die. At ninety-five, Tobie Steinhouse reread letters and newspaper clippings she'd kept for decades. She was choosing articles praising her work and photos of her exhibits to fill her designated shelf space in Canada's National Archive. Perhaps her interiority is one of the things that made her an artist. It certainly defines her beautiful paintings and prints, which will remain in galleries around the world long after the virus is less lethal. Untethered, we were all doing the same – trying to hold on to ourselves as we defied our own irrelevance. I admired her pertinacity.

In her late hey-day, artist and writer Mary Meigs had the same determination. I met her in 1975 when Nicholas was six and ran into our house in Richelieu Place with his friends one afternoon to say they'd accidentally broken the new neighbour's window. When I suggested they ring the bell, say sorry, and that they'd pay to have it repaired, they confessed that in the past few weeks their ball had frequently landed on her balcony and they had repeatedly been to her door to get it back. She would be very angry, so please would I go with them. When I refused they mumbled to one another, picked a flower from the garden on the way, and soberly rang the bell again. And there was Mary – tall, lanky, her neck wrapped in a wool scarf, her eyebrows concealed by her white bang. Perhaps the flower cooled her anger. Or perhaps it was her quiet, salty sense of irony that made her smile vaguely at them as she laid down the new rules for the lane behind her house.

Next time their ball went astray they were not to ring her bell because they were disturbing her work. She would return it to them every so often, and only on those afternoons could they play what they began to call Mary's game. She thanked them for the flower, and a few days later came to tea. We talked about *Jane Eyre*, which she was illustrating, and work as life's main motivator. Born to wealth, she had learned work's discipline at the top of Philadelphia's social scale. I'd been primed at the bottom of Montreal's. I soon came to call her my favourite Puritan, for she was the only person I've known with more productive guilt than I have.

Mary was sixty-four when she published her first book, *Lily Briscoe.* By then she had begun to feel time's winged chariot hovering. Her body, she said, was already non-cooperative when she woke in the morning. Age had taught her that memory magnifies light to see more sharply than the human eye and she spent the next twenty years fixing her life on paper as Lily Briscoe had searched for hers on canvas in *To the Lighthouse.*

After she appeared in Cynthia Scott's Oscar-winning film, *The Company of Strangers*, people came up to Mary in Montreal restaurants and stopped her in the street. She blushed as she always did when attention was paid, but she loved the fame. Cynthia had given her the courage to say she was lesbian on the big screen and Mary grew bolder thereafter in recording her life, and to some extent those of her friends. "You are private," she'd say to me when she was short of material. I was certainly uneasy the first time she rang to ascertain the details of a dream I had innocently shared with her. She was adding it to her dream diary, which is now housed at Bryn Mawr College along with her other papers.

In those early years of our friendship, Mary's and Marie-Claire Blais's first years together in Montreal, we often went to movies and concerts. Mary recorded details of everything she heard and saw, what people told her, the antics of her cats, her bird sightings in the Eastern Townships. She wrote about the afternoon we canoed together through wetlands near the summer house she and Marie-Claire shared in Racine about forty miles from Sutton the day before she had a stroke. And she was intensely curious in a clinical way about what was happening to her body the day of the stroke when I sat with her at the University of Sherbrooke Hospital and helped her begin to move her left hand and arm again.

All the Meigses had strokes, she said. Now it was her turn. Even on that day she was taking notes for her next book. It may have been her training as a painter that made her examine details most of us never see, or dare to see. It was certainly her determination to listen to her own voice, and her curiosity and courage in recording it that made what she saw unique and important. She told me that if possible she was going to watch herself die. Graham Greene thought that writers have "a splinter of ice in the heart." As a young man in hospital for an appendectomy he had watched and listened to a mother wail over her dead child when everyone else in the ward put on earphones. He called what he did selfish, but it was really an act of artistic integrity. Like Mary, he knew "this was something which one day I might need."

There were great parties at Mary's house. As one unusually formal gathering broke up, Elizabeth Smart, who was in the city to launch a new edition of *At Grand Central Station I Sat Down and Wept*, decided it was too early for her to go to bed. So Mary and Marie-Claire insisted that I take her somewhere for a drink. No, they would not come. "Take her over to The Main," they said. Alan and I had visited her sister Jane Marsh in Cambridge that summer on our way home from Cape Cod and I supposed that was why I was singled out. I soon learned different. When I finally got Betty back to the Château Versailles Hotel about four in the morning, she had drunk so much that I couldn't get her to leave the car for another hour while she cried out her woes à la *Grand Central Station*. Mary just smiled deviously when I accused her of setting me up. She said she would add what I'd told her to similar stories she'd been saving about Betty, and changed the subject to life-writing.

While everything seemed to sharpen Mary's pen, she was not pleased with fictional records of herself, especially Mary McCarthy's in *A Charmed Life*. We agreed that it's difficult to see yourself as other people do. Ray Smith had written about Alan and me in *The Man Who Loved Jane Austen*. He hadn't been to Sutton at the time so it wasn't surprising that he got that house wrong. But I thought he got us wrong too, although a student we had in common spotted me immediately.

After all, we were not characters in fiction. We were living beings, and in this case his friends.

For me Ray's book raised the question of privacy. To whom do the facts of our lives belong? With everything posted on line these days, it's difficult to answer as Mary did, to ourselves. I'd spent enough time in archives reading other people's papers to know the answer was more complex. And so did Mary when challenged. As a biographer, the question had bothered me for decades. I'd found out so much about people's secret lives that I knew was enticingly publishable. But early on I had decided to hold back anything that didn't add to our understanding of literary and cultural history. This wasn't a matter of legality, except for parts of Max's biography. It was a moral judgment I excused by styling myself as a literary biographer whose job it was to understand the work's relation to the life. And perhaps, for all his curiosity about other people's lives, my respect for Graham's dignity as a writer and his various tests of my loyalty had helped me come to that conclusion. I would never be the kind of biographer that writer Janet Malcolm called a professional voyeur.

Ray avoided the question of privacy entirely by refusing to acknowledge *The Man Who Loved Jane Austen* as autofiction. Strange that. Whenever I'm on de la Montagne, "snow flurries drifting, gleaming in the Christmas lights," I think of Ray pausing on the sidewalk as Frank does in his novel to watch the mesmerized children at the old Ogilvy's window before going "down the spiral staircase to the bookstore" to find treats for his boys. But like all of us, Ray was a tangle of contradictions – a romantic whose marriage was in a mess when he wrote the novel, a loving father who fled Montreal when especially his younger son still needed him, a professor who was so nervous that he shook before every lecture, and so empassioned by the literature he was teaching that he brought tears to the eyes of students lucky enough to hear him read from Tolstoy or Flaubert.

Mary thought he should have written about the breakup of his marriage squarely, as autobiography. Fictionalized biography, she said, was unfair because unacknowledged, its victims can't answer back. She was greedy for the inner experience she found in autobiography and biography, memoirs, diaries, and collections of letters. And she well understood the tension between facts and the biographer's need to turn them into narrative, which can so easily slip into fiction. That was why she thought biography harder to pull off than autobiography, in which to her everything was allowable. If what she called her own truth included stories about her family and friends, not all accurate from their point of view, she wasn't concerned. "It doesn't matter at all," she said. "Whatever I do, Virginia Woolf will have already done."

I wonder what Mary would have thought about the situation I found myself in recently with Tobie Steinhouse, whom she knew better than I did since they had been students together in the forties at the Art Students League in New York. Tobie survived COVID but then had a stroke that left her unable to read. Now at ninety-eight she'd had to move out of her house where she'd painted for sixty years, looking through her net-hung studio window across Côte Saint-Antoine Road in Westmount to Murray Park. Season after season that view had been her muse, the studio her private place. There beside her paints and easel and hundreds of her pictures and prints, she had kept old letters and scribbled thoughts among the other things she couldn't give up just yet. Then suddenly she could not read, and was instantly disjoined from what she had stashed to keep her company in old age. It was even more unnerving than being dislodged.

As a biographer I was used to reading people's letters. But my dead writers were beyond the violation Tobie felt as her family, however lovingly and necessarily, raked through her storehouse of memory. Still, she hadn't finished sorting her letters for the National Archive. Did she want me to read them to her? So private a person, she hesitated. So protective she said she could do it herself. Most were personal, she allowed, and shouldn't go to the Archive. Then one afternoon when we had gone to the house to take some paintings to her new sheltered apartment she suddenly said, "Yes." We'd spent a few summers decades ago in Sutton sitting silently in a field at the top of Schweizer's Hill while, looking in one direction she painted, and looking in another I wrote. But had our roles now been reversed would I have said yes even out of necessity, or just had everything shredded?

So we began, in 1946. The first bundle was from Anne Savage, a member of Montreal's Beaver Hall Group of women painters and Tobie's well-known teacher at Baron Byng High School. She had prized Tobie's talent and her letters were warm and supportive, encouraging a young student toward what her life might become because of her skill. And later when she was successful, Anne said that looking at Tobie's work made her understand the significance of using natural light in her own. How wonderful, I thought, for both student and teacher.

Until that day the thousands of private letters I'd read had passed through the hands of curators and cataloguers before they found their way to me. Here Tobie's hands and mine were both holding her letters, and her eyes were following the words through mine. I'm not sure how she felt as I read. But I do know that for me this was very different from reading Trekkie and Leonard's letters in the Sussex archive, or Graham's in the Harry Ransom Center in Texas, or Max's in our London flat. And something else. Having spent so much time reading private letters, I had long ago begun to destroy my own papers. Tobie's trust in the face of her vulnerability made me rethink Mary Meigs's insistence that shredding personal letters was suicidal that, as she said, "every woman's memory adds to the recorded chronicle of women's history."

Still, like Jane Eyre and Lily Briscoe, Mary was born with a sense of her own right. It was one of the things that intrigued me about her since I had little for myself, which may be why other people's lives so fascinate me and why until now I have hardly ever said "I" in print. Mary had a fine eye for the tapestry of every day's insignificant detail and an entirely unsentimental pen, but her insistence on giving her own evidence came as well from her upper-class confidence and her guilty need to justify the inherited wealth that allowed her to devote herself entirely to her work, something she thought being lesbian also helped her to do.

Caught like everyone by COVID restrictions, I should have been writing about Jean Ross, the real Sally Bowles. Her name has been linked to Christopher Isherwood's for decades, and she was not the woman Isherwood portrayed in *Goodbye to Berlin*, or the vamp of the many stage productions of John Van Druten's *I Am a Camera* and its musical adaptation as *Cabaret*. Like Bowles, she was an actor. She was also a highly intelligent journalist, a film critic, a translator, and the mother of one of Claud Cockburn's children who became a well-known barrister and wrote detective novels as Sarah Caudwell. An active member of the British Communist Party, she spent most of her life working toward social change in unacknowledged ways. When the tabloids rang her with each revival of Isherwood's story to ask how many men she'd slept with, Ross would tell them about Berlin in the thirties, about the unemployment, the poverty, the Nazis marching through the streets and then, depending on their response, hang up or continue to lecture them.

Instead, I found direction during the pandemic in writing things I hadn't said at the time about the people whose biographies I'd already published. Some were stories those people told me that on second thought I found more interesting than I had at first; some had to do with how I came to write their lives. Like everyone, I needed to hold on to my own narrative thread as I listened to the pandemic mephitis that flooded the media. What I didn't know when I started was where being my own reader would lead me.

I thought it important to say where I came from because the position of a biographer colours the work. But things look different at other times and I found I wasn't much good at self-revelation. Nonetheless, autobiographical questions arose. In *To the Lighthouse*

Virginia Woolf has James conclude that "nothing was simply one thing." Neither is anyone simply one person. As a biographer I had considered how individual lives connect to each other. How did my own connect with the lives I'd written? How was I changed by living in those other lives and by what I was doing while I was writing – mothering, teaching, and being a wife? And there were people I hadn't written books about who had influenced my writing, like Vincent Brome, who helped with publishing advice, and Mary in our lengthy discussions about life-writing. And Sigrun Bülow-Hübe, who told me her stories with such painterly detail that when I went to Stockholm I was able to find my way from the central bus station to Kökbrinken without a map. And those stories, so generously given, had come to me with the best directive for a biographer – record them without embellishment or you'll lose their truth.

A few days after she died, her older sister, Gunlög, rang in the middle of the night weeping because no one at Sigrun's house had answered the phone. "I forgot she's dead," Gunlög said. I'd never spoken to her before. Her English was spotty and my Swedish was very limited but she was a poet and needed words in whatever language. She continued to telephone when she couldn't sleep and to ask, "Yudi, please tell me a story." So to her I told the stories Sigrun had told me for the first time. Gunlög would laugh in their memory, then say, "Thank you, I have enough stories now," and ring off like a child closing her bed-time book.

Locked in a motionless present, I was not surprised that the wistful pull of London, where Alan and I spent so many years writing together, was irresistible. His death was like losing limbs I continue to feel, and adjusting one's balance is more than merely practical. Even to think about the British Library charged me with intellectual energy. To lunch with our friends at Vincent's table, then meander as we often did across the squares of Bloomsbury and down through the Inns of Court to smell the river on one of those afternoons which anyone who knew London in those years will remember to the end of their days, to duck in from the roar of traffic to a matinee or to look at pictures in the Courtauld, to meet for dinner at the Savile or eat on Lamb's Conduit Street at Ciao Bella and talk late in the evening, or wander through Hampstead where we lived when Nicholas was young and across the Heath where he learned to walk – these are things that gave shape to life and fuelled my writing. Nostalgia? Sure. With no objective future the past is lively.

Anyone who has seriously taken up a pen knows that you lose yourself in writing. It may be an unintentional part of the biographer's purpose. But only when I began to write about how London had pulled me toward biography did I fully realize the self I'd found in the complex give-and-take of the biographical process – what Mary might have called the paradoxical hitch.

I was an unsophisticated young woman when Graham handed me that first martini. Did it bother me that he was such a trickster? Then only as an amusing quality to be guarded against. When I came to appreciate it as part of his novelist's talent, it made a good story. At the time I thought getting to know him a privilege, and I still do. Only later did I realize that my work might be helping him.

I had an eight-year-old son when I went to the *Encounter* office in London and was given a pencil to rewrite a paragraph of "Looking for the Third Man" but I was still so professionally uncertain that my hand was shaking. I was certainly proud when I saw the journal with my name on its indigo cover at the newsstand outside Hampstead Tube Station. But it was not until I got to know Max that I began to feel that I knew what I was doing. I must have been in my mid-forties when Elizabeth Bowes-Lyon waited on the phone for me to write myself into *Reflections*. Of course, one is not necessarily a writer by wanting to be one and, as Mary Meigs said about herself as a painter, when I started I didn't know how much painful ground there was to cover between the beginning and the becoming.

Young women are more certain of themselves today, and much bolder in pushing themselves forward. They think differently about themselves in part because my generation taught our daughters to speak up and our sons to listen to what they said. My one advantage when I began to write was that I knew silence, a primary skill for a biographer. In a way I had been trained to it all my life, as a child to be seen and not heard and as a woman to defer to men in every sphere. Yet I've never thought I was not equal to a man, although I've always felt like an outsider. Even now I ask people questions that allow me to look through their eyes rather than confide my own secrets. Vincent used to say people told me their stories because they trusted me. But I knew they talked because I listened. And perhaps the people I was writing about thought I wouldn't gossip in London. I was always leaving for Montreal, and the Atlantic did put a distance between their secrets and my pen.

Did I know when I got permission to publish Trekkie and Leonard's letters how unconfident and divided Trekkie had been as a painter? I suppose I did about a year into the project. Then I thought her angst the result of the war and her domestically overburdened marital arrangement. Looking back I now understand it as common to most professional women, including myself. When Dadie Rylands told me that Trekkie said Lily Briscoe got it wrong, that a woman could be an artist and a mother, I thought, good for her. But in her diary she wrote about how hard it was to leave her domestic self outside the Blue Ark Leonard made for her because he knew she needed solitude.

Trekkie's complicated struggle to paint was not the same as Vincent's to write himself a living wage, or Graham's hunger to succeed in his early years. It was more like Charlotte Haldane's difficulty after she left JBS and the Party. Charlotte was much more cocksure than Trekkie, but the size of their output was comparable and their legacies were similar. Until *Love Letters* was published Trekkie was a small footnote in the Bloomsbury story. And in all her obituaries Charlotte was written off as little more than the talented but irritating first wife of J.B.S. Haldane.

When I discovered that close to her death Charlotte had written and circled inside the back cover of her Bible, "Que suis-je?" I knew I'd found a rhetorically neat ending for her biography. But I don't think I knew that using her question as my last line was such a powerful slap at the society that had belittled her for being a talented woman, at JBS and his family for how she'd been treated, and at Harry Pollitt and the British Communist Party. Without realizing what I'd done I had written a feminist ending. Alan Bennett would say I'd found myself in the writing. I think what I found was more nuanced, and important. Most people use, or are allowed to use, very little of their resources. With Charlotte's unanswered question I'd also asked what she might have been, and by extension what the women of her generation – and my own – might have done with their lives given more encouragement and fewer obstacles.

Living with Charlotte and Trekkie for a while had turned my head politically feminist. As Virginia Woolf put it, "when you write of a woman, everything is out of place – the accent never falls with a woman where it does with a man." Decades ago Mary Meigs reminded me of this when she insisted on the importance of listening to her own voice. In lockdown that's what you have to do – listen to yourself. For me that meant rethinking what I'd written and because of the time-lapse seeing it differently. In a couple of places I was offended by myself, and in many others saw how I could have done better – but improvement is always learned through hard work. In *Body Parts* Hermione Lee says biography is "a process of making up, or making over" and that for the biographer there is always "the internal tussle between 'making up' and 'fact,' or 'making over' and 'likeness.'" In finally hearing my own voice I came to realize the biographical process is reciprocal. As I tussled with "the making up or making over" of other people's lives, my likeness was made over too.

ooo

In a recent out-of-lockdown dream I picked up the .22 rifle my father brought us when we built our house in Sutton. His younger sister had used it for target practice and he said we might need it in the country. There were coyotes on the mountain and bears in the woods and we had no close neighbours. It never shot straight and, since Alan often used it to scare deer away from his rows of vegetables, it soon had no bullets. But in my dream I took it from its hiding place and shot Cerberus. "Can you do that?" I asked my sleeping self in astonishment and answered, "Well I did!" Somehow I'd been in Hades and out safely, with the past and future intact. I woke laughing at the irony of life itself.

"Husband your resources," Alan used to quote his maternal Winnipeg grandmother, Helen Tocher Townsend, as saying. She had come from Folla Rule, a hamlet in Scotland not fifty miles as the crow flies from Ferryden, the fishing village of my father's paternal family, the Coulls. She had trained as a midwife at the Royal Edinburgh Infirmary, the architectural model for my Royal Victoria Hospital. In Winnipeg she and the obstetrician father of Margaret Ann Elton, Alan's first wife, had delivered a generation of babies, including Alan and his four siblings. In the Adamson family old Bjornson's last words were remembered as: "Make sure the afterbirth comes away clean." Was what he said a habitual, semi-conscious directive to Alan's grandmother? Or was he thinking of a clean birth into another life for himself? Too bad there's no such easy solution for us today.

Downtown Montreal is no longer the centre of the world, as Bruce Trigger used to call it. After the night I came out of a nearby cinema from seeing *Murders in the Rue Morgue* and found Ontario Street had turned into avenue du Musée in the midnight mist, things seemed to change pretty fast. Children can still drink cocoa on Mountain Street (now de la Montagne, expunging Bishop Mountain's name from Montreal's history) but not as young Nicholas used to most afternoons at the Coffee Mill with chocolate whipped cream on top. By the time he went to university, that Hungarian indulgence had moved to Toronto, along with many patisseries and prize-winning restaurants. The lively jazz bars from which people used to spill out onto the sidewalk as often as not singing Renée Claude's "Sur la rue de la Montagne" have closed, the young poets and chansonniers decamped east to reinhabit the streets from which my generation moved downtown. They've made new cafés and restaurants for themselves and turned St Lawrence Boulevard (now boulevard Saint-Laurent but still called The Main) into the spine of the city centre. Old downtown is now inhabited by anonymous high-rises, expensive museum blockbusters, and bacchanalian festivals. Only one real café remains, a warm Iranian hangout where my office mate Yvonne Saleh and I often go for tea poured over rose petals. She too is an old downtowner and lives close by with her husband, George, in a beautiful hundred-year-old faux-Renaissance building.

There are now concerts to be heard at the bottom of du Musée where Bourgie Hall's back-lit Tiffany windows bear testament to the stories of that building's earlier occupant, Erskine and American United Church. The figures in those windows look west to the museum's original building on Sherbrooke Street where the little man Antony Gormley named "VI" stands naked against the elements, his head tilted upward for mercy. Close by there are still dinners to be had on white table cloths, but not in many places. After a concert with Jane Stewart, a neuroscientist and long-time downtowner who lives at the top of du Musée, we often eat at Il Cortile, a restaurant with tables set outside in the beautifully restored passage behind one of Sherbrooke Street's last standing blocks of limestone townhouses. Or we go to L'Autre Saison on Crescent Street in what was Lord Mount Stephen's original townhouse. That restaurant backs onto the lane between it and Drummond Street where, further down, Mount Stephen built the mansion for himself that eventually became the Mount Stephen Club. It was there that Alan slipped his Mexico City telephone number into the bodice of my first wedding dress. The club is now a hotel that recently served me a watery martini and has gold-plated taps in the ladies' loo.

Richelieu Place has remained more or less the same, although most of its thirty-three houses have been gutted and rebuilt inside. The 1925 arches off de la Montagne and du Musée have been replaced, albeit with exact replicas, and the old heating system that supplied warmth and hot water to us via a marvel of pipes running from a boiler room in the back alley up through the central garden has fallen to individual electric furnaces. But in my basement there is still a steel plate that allows entry to one of the original concrete tunnels through which the compound's cold water pipes run. Its floor is a pebble stream and by April every year it has a couple of inches of clean water running through it off the mountain at the top of du Musée. At our plumber's suggestion Alan had it tested when we bought our house and added it to his whisky for decades.

Across du Musée from Richelieu Place lives the artist Barbara Steinman. During the IRA bombings in London thirty years ago we found ourselves beside one another on a plane to Montreal. Heathrow had been closed the day before because of a bomb scare and we had both been rescheduled and were nervous. We got to the end of the runway then screeched to a stop. There was an extra suitcase on board and we had to stay seated in the locked plane while every bag was taken out of the luggage compartment to find the offender. Two frightening hours later Barbara and I ordered whisky and talked our way across the Atlantic to discover on landing that we lived almost opposite one another. A couple of years ago we made a low wall of old red bricks in the parking area behind her building. She'd found them in her furnace room. One stamped Meteor, another Fallston, and another La Prairie dated back over a hundred years. We'd imagined a secret garden there for a long time and planted daffodils inside the wall toward the yellow of spring. But early one summer morning last year a bulldozer was sent by the building's new owner to destroy our green urban effort for lucrative parking space.

So now my digging is confined to Sutton where the land has its own rhythms, and to the internet, where I continue to unearth Jean Ross's life in the twenty-first-century way of doing research. Cigarette in hand, she'd be on the front line against climate change and in this different era not be stained with Isherwood's naughty ink. But I am not a presentist and with her life I'm on dangerous biographical turf. Although her eye was always on injustice, opinions have changed as the times have, and what was then acceptable argument is now, like many things, said to be off colour. And perhaps so am I. After my generation's hard work toward intellectual freedom and social justice, things aren't going so well. Still, I think it's better to keep trying to remember the lines than to dismantle the set and switch off the lights.

Acknowledgments

I began this book in pandemic isolation when I should have been writing something else. But things don't always go the way you think they will. I want to thank Elaine Bander for encouraging me to go on with *Ghost Stories* once I'd started; her help en route was indispensable. Barbara Steinman, whose wisdom continues to astonish me, talked me through many rough patches. Tobie Steinhouse kindly trusted me with her personal letters. And my exemplary son Nicholas has been, as always, generous with his time and comments.

Thanks also to Mary Boulle, Pierre Boulle, Philip Cercone, Alexandra Clark, Ira Coleman, Mette Coleman, Diane de Kerckhove, Drew Duncan, Eva Echenberg, Julia Elton, Richard Greene, Sarah Jardine-Willoughby, Peter Lebensold, Jane McWhinney, Luke Reid, Yvonne Saleh, Amelia Sargisson, Jane Stewart, Adam Symansky, Judy Symansky, Irene Szylinger, and MQUP's anonymous reader A1.

Works Cited

In the preceding pages I have quoted small pieces from the following texts:

Page ix Richard Holmes, *This Long Pursuit* (London: William Collins, 2016), 6.

Page xi Alan Bennett, *The Lady in the Van*, Final Screenplay, Scriptsavant.co.

Page 7 Ian McEwan, *Atonement* (Toronto: Vintage Canada, 2002), 182.

Page 22 T.S. Eliot, "The Wasteland," *The Complete Poems and Plays* (New York: Harcourt, Brace & World, 1971), 47.

Page 22 John Donne, "To His Mistress Going to Bed," *Oxford Anthology of English Literature*, vol. 1 (Oxford, UK: Oxford University Press, 1973), 1023.

Page 22 Marie-Claire Blais, *A Season in the Life of Emmanuel* (Toronto: Exile Classics, 2009), 4.

Page 40 Richard Greene, *Russian Roulette* (London: Little Brown, 2020), 496, 12.

Page 62 Leo Tolstoy, "Childhood," Project Gutenberg eBook of Boyhood, 2000 (https://www.gutenberg.org/files/2450/2450-h/2450-h.htm).
Pages 62–3 Pablo Neruda, "I Will Come Back" (https://www.babelmatrix.org/works/es/Neruda%2C_Pablo-1904/Yo_Volveré/en/34620-I_Will_Come_Back).
Page 64 Charles Dickens, *David Copperfield* (London: Bradbury & Evans, 1850), 38.
Page 93 Virginia Woolf, *Orlando* (St Albans, UK: Panther, 1997), 41.
Page 94 Virginia Woolf, *Mrs Dalloway* (Oxford, UK: Oxford University Press, 2000), 92.
Page 109 Virginia Woolf, *A Room of One's Own* (Harmondsworth, UK: Penguin, 1974), 18–19.
Pages 118–19 Virginia Woolf, *Orlando*, 177–8.
Page 161 Graham Greene, *A Sort of Life* (London: The Bodley Head, 1971), 185.
Page 162 Ray Smith, *The Man Who Loved Jane Austen* (Erin, Ontario: The Porcupine's Quill, 1977), 7.
Page 169 Virginia Woolf, *Orlando*, 195.
Page 169 Hermione Lee, *Body Parts* (London: Pimlico, 2008), 29.

I have also drawn from my own books, notebooks, and tapes:

Graham Greene and Cinema (Norman, Oklahoma: Pilgrim Books, 1984).
Graham Greene: The Dangerous Edge (London: Macmillan, 1990).
"Sigrun Bülow-Hübe: Living Design," Canadian Architecture Collection (Montreal: McGill University Library, 1997).
Charlotte Haldane: Woman Writer in a Man's World (Basingstoke, UK: Macmillan, 1998).
Love Letters: Leonard Woolf & Trekkie Ritchie Parsons 1941–1968 (London: Chatto & Windus, 2001).